Our Debt to Greece and Rome

EDITORS

GEORGE DEPUE HADZSITS, PH.D.

DAVID MOORE ROBINSON, PH.D., LL.D.

Der Ackerman. Der Altman.

Der Rychman. Der Schiffman.

HOLBEIN'S DANCE OF DEATH
Reproduced from Woodcuts in
FOGG ART MUSEUM, HARVARD UNIVERSITY.
See Notes 65–67.

LUCIAN
SATIRIST AND ARTIST

BY

FRANCIS G. ALLINSON, Litt.D.

COOPER SQUARE PUBLISHERS, INC.

NEW YORK

1963

Published 1963 by Cooper Square Publishers, Inc.
59 Fourth Avenue, New York 3, N. Y.
Library of Congress Catalog Card No. 63-10286

In Memoriam
BASILI LANNEAU GILDERSLEEVE

CONTENTS

[vii]

ILLUSTRATIONS

LUCIAN, SATIRIST AND ARTIST

LUCIAN
SATIRIST AND ARTIST

I. CREDENTIALS FOR THE
TWENTIETH CENTURY

L UCIAN'S right to a conspicuous place
in Greek literature might seem open to
challenge. Born into the barbarian world
under Roman sway, of foreign and humble
parentage, in the second Christian century, he
seems, in race, place and time, sufficiently remote from even the tradition of the great Attic writers. But, as a subject of the Roman
Empire, his civic passport was visaed in advance from Syria to Gaul, and his genius, keen
if not profound, was destined to naturalize him
intellectually as an Athenian.

The canon of classical Greek was, apparently, long since closed but he reopened it by
his dramatic contributions to the Satiric Dialogue. He claimed, and not without reason,
Aristophanes and Plato as his god-fathers. A
Syrian by birth he was only a self-made Greek,

and yet he came to write the best Greek prose known since the days of Plato and Demosthenes. His Attic style, although veneered upon the " Common " Greek of his day, has relatively few flaws. He was a satirist, at times a sophist,[1] but also an artist.

It is difficult to assign rank and grades of precedence except for the royal line of the greater literary Olympians. Even on the Olympus of mythology, as leaks out through Lucian's *Caucus of the Gods* and *The Tragical Zeus,* the father of the gods found himself, on occasion, at a loss in attempting to seat in proper order, along with the duly matriculated Twelve divinities, the half-gods and gods of doubtful pedigree, like the bastards Dionysus and Heracles; the " druggist " Asclepius; or the Egyptian Anubis with his golden snout. Lucian was not one of the Twelve Olympians! He was more of a Heracles using on the Hydras of his century, in lieu of a club, the stiletto of satire and, without the compulsion imposed on the demi-god, addressing himself gaily to the cleansing of Augean Stables of charlatanry and accumulating superstitions.

Some analysis is attempted below of the dominant qualities of style and of the versatile humour, which, apart from the content of his writings, give Lucian his place in literature. For a sympathetic understanding of him, however, it is essential to consider briefly in advance what ethical purpose inheres in his satire and what corrections we must make in appraising his generalizations, his judgments and his prejudices.

Lucian's approaches to life are two-fold. Adopted into the Graeco-Roman world he gives with verve a rehabilitation of Greek antiquity or, on occasion, is wholly of his own time, deriding, attacking contemporary life. We must continually verify our perspective, from Homer to Demosthenes, from Menander to Marcus Aurelius. In so far as we are able to isolate the universal from the ephemeral we may profit by his samples of human problems and even by his failure to solve them. For him, as a comedian, all the world was undisguisedly a stage and all men and gods a joint-stock company of players on it. He was not hampered by any petty unities of time or place. The " play " is the real thing. By his fantasy, his best gift, he galvanizes into life, with varying realism, the rôles of gods and men.

Satire is dangerous. It often distorts the

vision. The great satirists, however, not only add to the "gaiety of nations" but also, as a rule, clear the moral atmosphere. To those who doubt this Lucian will probably make less of an appeal.

In connection with his ethical aims it is to be remembered that Lucian was not a philosopher in any technical sense. He cannot be successfully identified, as a convinced believer, with any of the four orthodox creeds nor even with the Cynics or the Sceptics. He used several of them, when it suited his purpose, but abused them all. He was too negative, too intellectually impatient, or even superficial, to appraise the ultimate value in each of them. He was no Marcus Aurelius who, as man, kept unspotted the *toga virilis* of serene Stoicism which he had assumed already as a boy. Still less was he a contributor to constructive scientific knowledge, like his great contemporary Galen. Lucian was not constructive either in philosophy and ethics or in any field except literature. Even in his serious crusade upon shams and ignorance his satire was determined by the sophistic spirit of his age. And yet, although somewhat pock-marked for life by his early attack of "rhetoric," his rebirth as a literary

[6]

artist differentiates him from the chronic sophists and mere professional rhetoricians.

To turn from the negative to the positive
side of his character, he was, or claimed to be,
the Apostle of Free Speech, the Interpreter of
Common Sense to the rational minority of his
day. A professed conservator of ethical values,
as he understood them, he was a sincere crusader against shams, inherited or new — the
pagan gods; the complex of contemporary philosophies, including especially the cherished
imperial Stoicism; pretenders in history, and
other literary adventurers; hypocritical legacy-
hunters, and other parasites; vulgar collectors
of books and relics; and, above all, the superstitions, major and minor, of his time. But he
could not, or would not, distinguish between
the willful liar and the misguided fanatic. Occasionally, in his sweeping satire, he makes no
attempt to distinguish the blatant impostor
from the true representatives of a creed or
principle. At times he is apparently carried
away by personal enmity. At other times he
ostentatiously notes the contrast between the
true and the false. All this makes it as necessary as it is difficult to reckon in his personal
equation. The effort is worth while. Although

even the casual reader will find amusement on nearly every page of Lucian's best writings the student of human history may find much more. With the parallax once established, we may triangulate a cross section of one of the most vital centuries in the history of civilization.

A parallel drawn between the Age of the Antonines and the present Age of Science may seem irrelevant. Human reason, equipped with the dazzling gifts, beneficent and maleficent, of applied science, seems to rest secure above the flood. Pessimistic prophecies of a return of the Dark Ages seem sufficiently negligible. The flow of disciplined reason from Democritus and Aristotle to Darwin, from Hippocrates and Galen to Pasteur has been, for long intervals, retarded or turned backward, but not dried up. None the less the intelligentsia of today, as in the Age of the Antonines, finds itself unexpectedly isolated by a new flood of unreason. Spiritists and fundamentalists, communists and commercialists, quack " educators " and litterateurs, even " casters of horoscopes " threaten the dear-bought progress of the disciplined mind in matters ethical, political, artistic and intellectual; some by undisguised obscurantism, others, who confuse motion with " progress," by laying their uncharted courses back from accredited discipline, back towards the caveman. For many, or all, of these phenomena illuminating illustration may be drawn from Lucian's satires. Applied with due attention to perspective, his mordant strictures may prove a useful corrective in the bewildering complex of uncorrelated ideas and desires that run riot in our suddenly dislocated civilization.

Finally, for this introductory statement, it seems desirable to summarize in advance a purely pragmatic appraisal of Lucian's contributions to literature and life, as reflected in his vogue among his own contemporaries and in his influence, conspicuous though intermittent, exerted upon subsequent generations.

Just how much or how little real effect his satires and polemics may have had upon contemporary thought and action is matter for conjecture, supplemented by some inferences from his own statements. He represents himself at the age of forty as prosperous and honoured. He undoubtedly drew large audiences. But there is no inevitable sequel, for ill or for good, to the words of a speaker or writer. Lucian contributed, perhaps, to the overthrow of the Olympic hierarchy but pagan orthodoxy

was already on the wane. He also mocked at
the crude superstitions of his time, but in his
Lie-Fancier, for example, the trusted physician, the gouty householder and the long-
bearded philosophers, Peripatetic, Stoic and
Platonic, continue undismayed their exchange
of supernatural marvels.

In the two centuries, the third and the fourth
of our era, which immediately followed the
death of Lucian, he seems to have enjoyed only
a precarious popularity. The pagans had little
cause to love him, for he had done his best to
shatter their idols; and the Christians, as they
began to emerge from obscurity, while borrowing on occasion his darts against paganism,
must be cautious that these same arrows were
not winged with their own feathers. Obviously,
they could not be in sympathy with the essential outcome of his agnosticism. Only a few
free spirits outside of the struggle between
paganism and Christianity were then " en état
d'entrer sans arrière-pensée dans ses sentiments." [2]

In the Middle Age, when an external Christianity was securely enthroned, Lucian again
became available and superficially popular.
The most scrupulous adherents of the church

could anticipate inconvenient criticism by de-
nouncing him in advance as a blasphemer, liar
and atheist and then proceed to enjoy him and,
in a crippled fashion, to imitate him. Notwithstanding his tincture of antichristian Epicure-
anism, his ethical views often marched with
Christian asceticism in emphasizing the vanity
of riches and the brevity of mortal life. Added
to this, Lucian's crushing ridicule of pagan
divinities was always a convenient asset to
church partisans who managed to ignore the
ultimate deduction which denatured the very
spirit of divinity itself.

With the Revival of Learning, however, Lucian came into his own, both as a literary artist — his real *métier* — and as a stimulating
critic of human life. The eager minds of the
Renaissance could assimilate the charm of his
brilliant style and fantasies and apply to their
own environment his crusading spirit. The crop
of imitators grew apace. In pictorial art Lucian
originated or transmitted from antiquity suggestions for the great artists of Europe. His
undisguised influence in literature is still more
wide reaching, and his influence, now subtle,
now open, upon thought and controversy, from
Erasmus on, permeated the reawakened spirit

of the age. He was a natural born ally for the Humanists against the Obscurantists.

By the middle of the sixteenth century, however, the literary satire inspired by Lucian developed a cross-current athwart the troubled waters of theological controversy. From the coarse-grained cartoons of Rabelais and the charming humour of Hans Sachs the stream flowed on, almost uninterrupted, into and through the seventeenth and eighteenth centuries, tossing on its surface the Lucianic flotsam, easily identified and often actually stamped with his name. The favourites among Lucianic motifs in this period were the mendacious verities of the *True Story* and the *memento mori* of the *Dialogues of the Dead*.

Although Lucianic imitations and suggestions were not lacking in the nineteenth century, M. Croiset [3] records and explains a temporary interruption of the closer community of thought that bound the men of the Renaissance to Lucian. " Le développement de la science et des méthodes scientifiques, qui est la fait caractéristique du dix-neuvième siècle, nous a peu à peu habitués à traiter sérieusement la plupart des choses dont Lucien parlait avec légèreté. Nous ne rions plus des aventures de Zeus, ni de la folie ascétique de Pérégrinus. L'histoire est par nature tout l'opposé de la moquerie. Elle cherche la raison des choses, ce qui lui ôte l'envie d'en rire." This penetrating observation, made by the accomplished French interpreter of Lucian in the last quarter of the nineteenth century, might seem even more true of the first decades of the present century. Now, both to applied Science and to misapplied Religion is freely charged up the failure of civilization. Lack of confidence in each is jauntily expressed by journalistic straw-ballots. It is, to be sure, no time to " laugh and grow fat " but a sense of humour saves many a situation. Lucian's comic mask, one side serious, the other smiling sardonically, may prove valuable among the assorted " properties " of the twentieth-century stage.

II. AGE OF THE ANTONINES

LUCIAN lived through the greater part of the second century after Christ. This includes the age of the benignant Antonines. The stately " grandeur that was Rome " is reflected by him on many a page. The Greek Renaissance under Roman sway, with which the Emperor Hadrian had identified himself, is an item carried forward on the balance sheet of our combined " Debt to Greece and Rome."

One reminder of this Graeco-Roman aftermath of art is the temple of Olympian Zeus which, though originally projected 600 years before Lucian's time, was begun anew on a vast scale in the second century B.C. and finally dedicated under Hadrian when Lucian was a boy in Samosata. The grandiose and beautiful columns [4] still extant from this structure are a notable landmark in the Athens of today. When Lucian first arrived from the Orient he must have found the temple, in its fresh and stately splendour, the pride of the Athenians, and it helps us to an understanding of our versatile Syrian to think of him as habitually walking through this majestic precinct — a contemporary epitome of the combined civilizations of Greece and Rome. Among these still imposing ruins the visitor sits today at sunset and looks up at the Acropolis between the same columns, crowned with their acanthus capitals, while the violet light descends on the encircling mountains and imperceptibly blends the Athens of Theseus with all its later history. As compared with our outlook fewer centuries would subtend Lucian's vision but they would, after all, include the most vital epochs in Athenian history — the dim days of the ancient kings; the creative Hellenic period; the rule of Macedon; and the sway of Rome. And, more impressive than the modern caravans of visitors — students, tourists or diplomats — there would have been, in the near background of tradition or still actually passing, the long procession of pilgrims who had journeyed by Roman roads and swift galleys on business of statecraft, learning, pleasure or profit — merchants, captains and proconsuls; grammarians, poets and artists: Cicero and Brutus in their eager youth; Horace conning, in the already partially distorted pronunciation of the " Common " Greek,

[15]

the measures of Alcaeus and Sappho; Virgil, dreaming of some new grace for his *Aeneid;* Ovid like a revelling bee storing his own fragrant honey from Hymettus though destined, in the " trist " days to come, merely to sight the Acropolis from the Saronic Gulf as he sailed by despairingly to his distant exile; Pliny, the meticulous imperial official of Lucian's own day, pausing perhaps, *en retour* from Bithynia, to secure some Greek gem for insertion in the charming setting of his epistles; or — a vivid tradition at least to the Christians — Saint Paul as interpreter of " an Unknown God "; and, finally, the successive epiphanies of the imperial masters themselves, Augustus, Nero, Hadrian, Aurelius.

Lucian in Hadrian's Athens seems, in the foreshortened centuries, almost equidistant from the present day and from antiquity. He is essentially modern but through the highways and byways of what was antiquity to him, as well as to us, he walked with the nonchalance of an acclimated foreigner.

If we try to visualize the Graeco-Roman background, intellectual and social, for the age of the Antonines we are impressed by the large-mindedness, based on the serene consciousness of their own greatness, with which the Romans had from the first welcomed to their civilization the alien cultural elements offered by the newly-acquired Greek province. Already in the time of the young Cicero a " foreign university " training in the Greek schools of rhetoric and a mastery of the Greek language were normal additions to the equipment of young and ambitious Romans. Political life was subordinated to Rome but the Greek characteristics were not obliterated. Juvenal's " Graeculus esuriens," as contemptuous a generalization as " dago," had been sufficiently forestalled by Horace's diagnosis of the invincible vigour of " captured " Greece. And, when we come to Lucian himself, while he spares, in his *Led Philosophers*, no detail of the humiliations accruing to the hired Greekling, he is in reality endeavouring to spur men of his own profession to a nobler, independent life.

The record of this age is not crowded with names distinguished in Greek literature. Lucian himself, a foreigner, is the most conspicuous. Plutarch, gentleman and scholar and a loyal Greek citizen, had died about the time of Lucian's birth. In the Age of the Antonines, a notable rendezvous for scholars and visitors to

Athens was the hospitable villa of Herodes Atticus at Cephisia, near Marathon. Herodes, eminent as writer and teacher of rhetoric in Rome and at Athens, was drawn into official life through imperial favour; was administrator in 125 A.D. of the free towns in Asia Minor; and, in 143 A.D., was raised to the consulship by Antoninus Pius. His great wealth, inherited from his father, enabled him, however, to free himself from the trammels of office and to establish himself in luxury in his Attic country-place, devoting himself to his real ambition as an orator and, incidentally, from time to time, winning for himself public esteem, or graceless criticism, as the munificent donor of splendid structures at various sites. He is one of the few contemporaries actually singled out for praise by Lucian, who refers to the beneficent gift of the aqueduct that brought a pure water supply to the throngs of visitors at the Olympic Games.

Among distinguished guests at the Attic villa we can certainly think of Aristeides, famous as a rhetorician and a pupil of Herodes. Arrian, too, who makes his own " anabasis " from imperial business to the more difficult heights of literature, probably found a stimulus in the

coterie at Cephisia. It is recorded that he was
archon eponymous at Athens in the year 147/8.
Pausanias, the painstaking " Baedeker," has
much to say of the contemporary public mu-
nificence of Herodes and we need have little
hesitation in thinking of him as a guest at
Marathon. The loss of Appian's autobiography
leaves us in the dark about a possible stay in
Athens of this Greek historian of Rome, but
in regard to two Latin contemporary writers,
we know that they were much in Athens. Aulus
Gellius, indeed, the grammarian and author of
Attic Nights, enjoyed, as we are told, the friend-
ship and instruction of Herodes, though the
arid contents of his book seem to reflect the
parched days rather than the lovely nights of
the Attic country-side. The well-groomed
Apuleius might certainly have been a welcome
guest at the well-appointed villa and if we can
assume that our naturalized Syrian would also
have been *persona grata,* in spite of his bitter
crusade against imperial Stoicism, we might
imagine the two riding their respective mounts,
the *Asinus* and the *Golden Ass,* to stable them
at this same hospitable manger at Cephisia. Be
that as it may, we should need to assume
abundant tact on the part of the genial host to

[19]

reconcile the orthodox piety of a Pausanias or the devoted loyalty of Gellius to his teacher Peregrinus Proteus with the impatient agnosticism of Lucian or his bitter diagnosis of the charlatanry of the Cynic suicide.

Apart from literature in its narrower connotation, two men, conspicuous in the world's development of science, are contemporaries and we should like to bring them into actual juxtaposition with the others at the villa of Herodes. The great Ptolemy who lived and wrote in Alexandria, "the sister-university to Athens," could on occasion soar to his own stars in exquisite verse which is well worthy of its place among the choicest Greek epigrams. Whether Lucian could have known him either at Athens or later in Egypt is exceedingly doubtful but it is at least permissible, in this connection, to relieve Lucian of the authorship of the piece, *Concerning Astrology*, which has been included [5] among his writings. Lucian would not have been competent to write on astronomy but he would have been sure to rate astrology, in its narrowed, magical interpretation, amongst other unworthy superstitions. It flourished in the Orient and from the second century B.C., when the Hellenic spirit was waning, spread like a cancer through the Graeco-Latin world.[6]

The other great scientific contemporary, Galen, the legatee of Hippocrates and the forerunner of modern psychiatry, was Lucian's junior by a few years only. It is not improbable that they may have met in Athens on some occasion when Galen was journeying between Pergamum and Italy at the Emperor's behest. Lucian unfortunately, however, confines himself to contemptuous satire upon superstitious or incompetent medical contemporaries.

Marcus Aurelius himself touched at Athens in 176 A.D. on his way home from Egypt to Rome and if we may postpone the death of Atticus to the year 180, the very latest date allowed him, it would be in order to think of the Emperor as entertained at the villa of his favoured friend and former teacher. At any rate, if we were at liberty to collect all these guests at one time in one place,[7] we know that the imperial author of *The Meditations* would have been able to discuss in Greek either mathematics with Ptolemy, medicine with Galen, or literature and ethics with Lucian and the others.

This Age of the Antonines is replete with

interest. Material power centred at Rome and the attitude towards literature, philosophies and religions was very catholic — even superciliously tolerant if we except the occasional severity to the Christians. Imperial University professorships were established, throughout the more civilized parts of the Empire, for representatives not only of the Stoics but also for those of the three other officially recognized schools of philosophy — the Epicureans, the Academics and the Peripatetics, — while " Dissenters," like the Cynics and Sceptics, unpaid but unmolested, preached their doctrines outside the pale of the " established " systems.

Although the beneficent reign of Marcus Aurelius was to close amid the clash of arms and was darkened by misgivings, only too well grounded, in regard to his unworthy son and successor, such factors as make for an advancing civilization — literature, art, philosophy, mathematics and medicine — took on renewed life under the sunlight of imperial favour. As a mere boy Marcus Aurelius had put on the garb of a Stoic and throughout his life moulded his character by exemplifying the noble elements of self control and charity towards others — qualities not always equally predominant in this stern creed. The blot on his otherwise noble administration of the Empire is his reversal of the tolerant policy of Hadrian and Antoninus Pius towards the Christians. This seems out of keeping with the humane liberality of Aurelius, but it is likely that he divined, in Christianity's uncompromising rejection of all other faiths, the underlying menace to the State religion in which he actively believed. The contemptuous tolerance of the Christians expressed by an agnostic like Lucian, in his *Life's End of Peregrinus*, might well have seemed inadequate to the Emperor's sense of serious obligation.

As for religion in general, the wide-spread atheism of the first Christian century issued in this century in sporadic attempts to resuscitate the ghosts of old creeds or was supplanted by more novel attractions.

III. LIFE OF LUCIAN

FOR the details of Lucian's life we are thrown back upon the casual or explicit references to his career in his own writings. From his contemporaries or from later writers we obtain little or nothing[8] that is tangible. We do not know the exact dates of his birth and death but we are in a position to make a fairly clear sketch of some of the external facts of his life and we are able with reasonable certainty to fill in still more of the inner development of his mind and character.

Lucian was born, probably about 120 to 125 A.D.,[9] in Samosata on the Euphrates. This provincial town, capital of Commagene, the extreme northeast portion of Syria, was not without importance as commanding the passage of the Euphrates River on one of the great trade routes to the Orient. The district, first subjected to Roman control in 18 A.D., had, after various vicissitudes, been made by Vespasian permanently a province of the Roman Empire. The population, however, was mainly Syrian, and Lucian, with the semi-defiance usual with

" self-made " men, refers, now and again, to his
Syrian birth and barbarian mother tongue. His
Samosatan parents were poor but eager to place
their son in a calling suitable for a free-born
man. To decide on his career a family conclave
was held. From Lucian's *Dream,* an address
made to his own townspeople when, rich and
famous, he returned home on a visit, we get a
sufficiently vivid picture of the boy's Samosatan
environment and native endowment — at least
on his mother's side. His maternal grandfather
had been a statuary, apparently a modest sculptor and stone-cutter combined, and his mother's
two brothers followed the same calling. After
various propositions had been considered for
form's sake, the father of the family was given
an opportunity to express publicly his wife's
decision and, turning to one of the maternal
uncles, remarked that in *his* presence no other
master or career for the boy could be selected.
" So do you take him," the text goes on, " and
teach him to be a good worker and joiner of
stone and a sculptor; for he has in this, as you
know, native ability and cleverness. He drew
the inference from the way I used to play with
the wax. For, whenever I was let out of school,
I used to scrape the wax off my tablets and

model cows, horses or even humans, by Zeus,
— very life-like ones as father thought." Although the boy had been repeatedly flogged for
this maladministration of his writing materials,
his fond parents now deemed it prophetic of
his predestined artistic success. His apprenticeship to his uncle lasted, however, less than a
day. Using his chisel with more zeal than dis-
cretion the boy broke a marble slab, was well
flogged for it by his uncle, ran home sobbing to
his masterful mother and explained to her that
his uncle had already become jealous of his
budding talent. The outraged mother, with all
the acumen of a modern parent, sided at once
with her offspring against his preceptor, her
own brother, and, fortunately for posterity,
saved the boy for a wider career than that of
a local stone-cutter. The incident, however, is
indicative of part of Lucian's equipment. His
motifs drawn from plastic and pictorial art
have been often recorded. His comments on
actual sculpture and paintings extant in his
time are not without value and indicate, at
least, sincere sympathy with beauty of line and
composition. It is tempting to imagine that his
boyish efforts at modelling issued in the keen-
ness of perception and fidelity of outline char-

acteristic of the literary artist. It is tempting also, though perhaps too proleptic, to think of Hermes and Charon, or their Syrian congeners, together with sundry deceased Samosatans whose tombstone portraits he had seen in his uncle's marble yard, as already shaping themselves in his boyish imagination into the ghostly *dramatis personae* of after years.

Whatever his mental furnishing, the youth was sent forth, or went forth, to seek his fortune abroad. We must assume that his ambition was already stirring to make of himself a public speaker, advocate and rhetorician. Rhetoric kept the toll-gate on the highroad to fame in this second century. There were famous centres of rhetoric at Antioch; at Ephesus and Smyrna on the Ionian seaboard; and at Athens. But even Antioch was 160 miles from his native town. We do not know either his means of livelihood, or just how he obtained instruction, or his itinerary in these ten years of preparation. He left home poor in purse, hardly emancipated from his oriental garb, and still " barbarian " in speech, but he had somehow in these years succeeded in transforming himself into an incipient rhetorician and, far more important for his future career, had acquired so intimate a knowledge both of Greek classic literature and of the spoken vernacular that he would presently be able to surpass his Greek-born contemporaries in the current effort, successful with a few only, to recall to new life the Attic Greek.

It would be interesting to know whether some master, like Polemon, recognizing his ability, admitted the impecunious youth to his high-priced lectures, accepting his promising talent in lieu of coin. If so, Lucian has left no record of his obligation. In view of his subsequent development it seems likely that he picked up, here and there, such scraps as he could of technical knowledge but that his real disciplinary training was self-devised and eclectic. He was, in short, fortunate enough to have escaped the deadening effects of the formal pedagogy of the schools. His natural superficiality, evident enough to the end of his career in his attitude, for example, towards the philosophical systems, might, conceivably enough, have been more successfully concealed by perfecting himself in the conventional formulae of Rhetoric but he might also have been deflected from his true development as charming narrator and creator of Satiric Dialogues.

In the *Fisher* or *The Resurgent Philosophers,* Lucian defends himself against the angry ghosts who have heard in the underworld inflaming reports of the insulting sale of philosophers at auction. They have obtained a day's furlough from Hades and are here to punish him. They have taken to themselves his bitter ridicule and condemnation of contemporary charlatans who disgrace their " cloth." In the course of his defense Lucian says: " Where or when have I ever insulted you? I who have lauded you personally beyond measure and have lived in communion with the literature which you have left to posterity? Why, these very words that I am speaking, from what other source than from you did I receive them and, like a bee culling from flowers, transmit them to mankind? Nominally people envy me for my ' bouquet ' but in reality they admire you and your meadow for putting forth bloom so varied and of such multiform colours." It is evident enough that the Syrian youth, long before the date of this dialogue written in his best period, had familiarized himself with the Classic Greek, hampered, perhaps, only by the inaccessibility of the rarer books. He became an artist in literature not because of, but in spite of, intermittent practice as a lawyer or his successful career as a rhetorician.

As to the latter phase of his development we gain the best idea from his own account in the *Double Indictment*. This is an autobiographical résumé of what to Lucian himself seemed momentous in his own career. The metaphorical liaison with " Lady Rhetoric," it may be remarked, has been seized upon by literally-minded commentators as reflecting a real wedlock with a wife rich enough to furnish him with equipment for his war upon shams. As a matter of fact his two meagre allusions to his father, family and little son do not include even " brief mention " of an actual wife, although her existence is a not unreasonable inference.

The *Double Indictment* takes its title from two law-suits brought against Lucian: one by Rhetoric, for desertion; the other by Dialogue, for maltreatment. We are told that he had previously made a lucky match with a rich lady named Rhetoric, who now complains that whereas she had bought fine clothes to replace his oriental " caftan ";[10] had taught him fine Greek to replace his Syrian speech; had taught him, too, how to manage like a gentleman the folds of his robe and his flowing eloquence; had, finally, to please him, secured sailing reservations and had taken him abroad and travelled with him everywhere — to Italy, to Transalpine Gaul and back again — and had raised him to fame and fortune, yet he had in the end basely deserted her for a boon companion, named Dialogue.

"Dialogue," in turn, lodges formal complaint that this deceitful Syrian, freed by him from the degrading union with Lady Rhetoric, had maltreated him shamefully. "He has disfigured me," Dialogue urges, "beyond recognition. Taking advantage of our intimacy and of my unwary complaisance, he has forced me to masquerade in such strange guise that I no longer recognize myself as fit for Plato's Academe. He has hidden my honest countenance behind a leering comic mask out of which, despite myself, issued iambic jest and Cynic doggerel so that I am rated as an unclassified monstrosity like to nothing on earth or in the air. I can neither pace in prose nor mount on metre."

This flash-light picture, taken from within, is worth more than many external details, which we lack, to illuminate the real development of

the man. He does make, however, many scattered allusions to his career. His tour of the
provinces, as a rhetorician, was very successful.
He made a prolonged stay in Gaul, where he
received large pay as one of the " high-priced
Sophists."

As to Lucian's linguistic equipment outside
of Greek and Syrian, we have only negative
data. He lays no claim to a knowledge of Celtic
and, in fact, refers with satisfaction to a Gallic
philosopher, " who spoke Greek accurately."
He is usually accredited with only a meagre
knowledge of Latin and it would, in fact, be
difficult to demonstrate, from his writings, a
thorough-going familiarity with Latin literature.
His various visits to Rome, however, may well
have stimulated the versatile Syrian to perfect
his acquaintance with the imperial language
which he must have heard spoken in his boy-
hood, and a somewhat fluent, if superficial,
knowledge of the vernacular is implied, though
not proved, in his apology for an apparent break
in conventional usage, made, when already of
advanced age, in addressing the Emperor. Here
he throws in the jaunty remark: " If I am at
all expert in the speech of the Romans." [11] The
implied conclusion is: *As I think I am.* As he

would hardly learn to speak fluently in a foreign tongue when he was already an aged government official we must conclude that he equipped himself with Latin by the time he was first lecturing in Gaul. The methods and limitations of spoken communication through a complex of languages such as existed under the Roman Empire or, for example, under the late Austro-Hungarian Empire, constitute a not unimportant factor in the mechanism of human history. The wide-spread use of the " Common " Greek was an asset taken over by the Romans from Alexander's legacy. Many Romans, " from Emperor to clown," could use it readily, and travellers bent on business or pleasure doubtless employed, at a pinch, either this " Common " Greek itself or some ruder compromise as a *lingua franca*.

There is, however, nothing to indicate that Lucian employed any other language than Greek in his public speeches. Even in the autobiographical address, made to his Samosatan townspeople, far from reverting to his native Syrian, he ostentatiously displays, along with other *indicia* of his success in life, his adroit use of the Greek language sprinkled with literary allusions. Incidentally, it is suggestive that these allusions, however superficial, were intelligible on the banks of the Euphrates.

Thus at the age of forty Lucian found himself possessed of no little fame. Doubtless he exaggerates this in his autobiographical boastings. The Roman Empire was large and there was other more important news for the couriers to carry along the far-flung post-roads. But as things went in this second century he was an unqualified success as travelling rhetorician and show-lecturer. He could, as occasion demanded, deliver an *Encomium on a Fly;* a biographical appraisal like his *Herodotus;* or indulge in philological fooling, as in *The Suit of Sigma versus Tau.*

From Gaul and Italy he apparently returned to Ionia by way of Athens. In the first years of the rule of Marcus Aurelius he was again in Syria, and in 162 or 163 A.D. at Antioch he saw Lucius Verus, the Emperor coadjutor. It has even been suggested that he had resumed for a time at Antioch his interrupted career as advocate. After this, it would seem, he made his final emigration to Athens, taking with him his father and his family.

In 165 A.D. Lucian was at Corinth and also at the Olympic Games for the third or the fourth time, according as we assume that the self-immolation of the Cynic Peregrinus near Olympia took place in this year or in 169 A.D. From this time on Lucian apparently made Athens his headquarters and we may refer to this period his best literary activity. It is, indeed, well-nigh impossible to give a wholly satisfactory chronology for his writings but we are apprised by his own high-sounding words of the psychological crisis that supervened. " Tired of the shifting business of the turbulent forum and the cloying applause of the masses " he turns in contempt from rhetoric " to take his pleasure with Dialogue either in the Academy or in the Lyceum." Whenever this rebirth took place, it was the principal event in his life. In the development of the Satiric Dialogue he found his true career as literary artist. It was an intellectual and moral emancipation. The flowery fetters of rhetoric fell off; [12] he ceased to coquet with philosophy. The artist remained.

Well-to-do and well known, he composed for many years. In his old age, however, — the exact date is unknown — we find him again, either by reason of pecuniary need or from a restless desire for increasing his fame, turned into a circuit show-lecturer and in his earlier

manner suing for public favour through dec-
lamations and readings. Some genuine pieces
which may have been written at this time
would be inaptly ascribed to his more virile
manhood. And, finally, when the curtain falls,
we take leave of this life-long non-conformist
installed in orthodox security as a government
official in Egypt with a good salary drawn from
the imperial treasury.

IV. EXTANT WRITINGS: FORM AND CONTENT

THERE are at least eighty-two titles listed under Lucian's name. Of these, six pieces are certainly not genuine. Twenty-eight more have been called in question by expert authorities who are, however, by no means in complete agreement. With all of these deducted there would remain only forty-eight but, by a reasonable, though composite, consensus of opinion at least sixty [13] may be treated as genuine. Some of these fifty to sixty pieces are very short. Other titles, however, represent groups so that the total amount attributed to Lucian occupies thirteen hundred and seven pages of (the Teubner) Greek text. [14]

Lucian, best known for the development, if not the creation, of the Satiric Dialogue and, next to that, for his skill as a story-teller, makes large use of other forms to suit varying content. There are a number of short epideictic pieces used, perhaps, as prefaces or " curtain-raisers " to longer readings or lectures;

there are many writings of a hortatory or didactic, argumentative or polemical, and, occasionally, of a biographical character; some
pieces are constructively or even actually in the
form of letters. He is not always severely careful about preserving a consistent form but injects, for example, into some of his best dialogues argumentative or narrative digressions
to reënforce his theme. These insertions, which
dam back, as in Plato, the current of the dialogue, occasionally contain some of his choicest
satire.

There are also two tragico-comic poems
which find tentative recognition as Lucianic
compositions, to be accepted, perhaps, by referring them to his closing and less virile years.
Finally, there are in the Greek Anthology
forty-two epigrams attributed to Lucian. Only
a few of these seem, from internal evidence, to
suggest his authorship. There is, however, no
reason to assume that the versatile Syrian may
not, from time to time, have experimented, like
many others of mediocre poetical facility, with
this time-honoured and popular literary form.

It is not safe to be dogmatic about the chronological order of all of Lucian's writings. Con-
tradictory and plausible arguments have been

adduced, in the case of many pieces, for a varying sequence.[15] It is safe, however, to accept Lucian's own testimony, in the autobiographical *Double Indictment*, concerning the intellectual crisis through which he passed in transforming himself from a not unsuccessful rhetorician into an artist of a higher and more specialized type. The humourous parable concerning Lady Rhetoric and Dialogue, the substitute partner, does not disguise the seriousness of the decision which confronted him when he came to the parting of the ways. The important point is that he knew and believed in his own artistic powers. His desertion of Lady Rhetoric does not imply the obliteration of his early rhetorical self-training, nor even of all of his sophistic tendencies, but it does imply that he had the courage to turn from a fashionable and lucrative career to work out his own genius in his own way. It is evident that his best productivity was subsequent to this change which was, of course, a progressive one. Feeling his way under the influence of Attic Comedy, he passed into a phase where the " ironic and treacherous grace " of the Cynic Menippus, inlaid upon his Platonic and other studies, openly furnished him with suggestions for many of his most successful dialogues. He then entered upon a still more advanced period when his maturing powers came to perfection and his wit could reflect more clearly the brilliancy of the Old Comedy. He could now — in the *Double Indictment* — review his career with pardonable pride and claim Aristophanes and Plato as his two god-fathers. All the writings that secured his fame and that were destined to exert so great an influence upon distant generations, belong to these mature periods, but, in the case of several pieces, including some of the polemics, it is hazardous to assign even an approximate date. When he was, perhaps, nearly sixty there would seem to have been a cessation of his productivity. His latest writing and his epideictic addresses, resumed in his old age, offer little that is characteristic of his best period. Not only the waning of his powers but also his position as an imperial official hampered his wit and his freedom of speech.

Whatever citations space will allow, in the following chapters, must serve a double purpose, illustrating some phase of activity under discussion — such as his crusades upon shams and superstitions — and also the qualities of his style.

Coming as a *novus homo,* so to say, into the peerage of Greek literature, Lucian stored his mind with the " classics," from Homer to Menander. By reading, memorizing, citing and even imitating he perfected his Attic Greek and familiarized himself with the content of much of the greatest Hellenic prose and poetry. Some writers, doubtless, were less accessible than others; in some the subject-matter made less appeal to him and it is not surprising, perhaps, to note, for example, conspicuous omission of several of the great Lyric poets. To various others, moreover, he makes only perfunctory reference. He brought to his task his own contribution of native wit, esprit and imagination, and, after his tentative apprenticeship, he struck out on his own path. It is no small tribute to this Syrian foreigner that any résumé of Greek literature must be extended so as to include his name. He remained, to some extent, self-conscious in his brilliant and painstaking application of his art. His barbarian extraction, to which he repeatedly refers, only heightened his frank satisfaction in his indebtedness to Plato, Demosthenes, Herodotus and other models. His rejoinder to the " resurgent philosophers " in the *Fisher* is explicit. Although

[41]

he does not specify one only as his " Master,"
he is speaking directly to Plato when, like
Dante, he acknowledges the source of the
" beautiful style that has done honour " to him.

However difficult it may be to isolate the
verbal mechanism of style from the spirit and
qualities that it embodies, it is peculiarly necessary in Lucian's case. " Proper words in proper
places " is the dictum of Swift who is, probably, the most " Lucianic " of all of Lucian's
modern legatees. To attain to this propriety
the Syrian not only had to learn the language
in question but he had the far more difficult
task of joining with his contemporaries in the
ambitious project of remoulding a chaotic vernacular into a worthy instrument of grace and
power. The " Atticists " of the day were attempting this task by the purely artificial
method — *a priori* futile, it might seem — of
veneering classic Attic upon the " Common "
Greek which, in the course of some four hundred years, had deviated widely, both in form
and in vocabulary, from the Greek of Demosthenes and Menander. Lucian accepted the
challenge of the current fad — he was not, in
fact, in a position to do otherwise. He, too,
strove to erect the " Common " Greek into a

thing of life. He was not a Virgil or a Dante,
able to break in rebellious native colts and
harness them obedient to the guiding rein of
supreme poetry, sweeping to victory the vehicle
itself of perfected speech. But he worked his
own miracle. He succeeded, where most of his
contemporaries failed, in writing an almost
perfect Attic and, far more important, in
achieving a flexible, if not flawless, style of
great charm and clarity.

When this mastery of the best practicable
medium of language was once attained his native endowment had free course. He enfran-
chised himself, at the proper time, from the ab-
solute despotism of epideictic rhetoric but he
also refused to spend his life in polishing and
repolishing his grammatical weapons. Confi-
dent enough in the approximate correctness of
his own diction he could even venture on occasion, as in his *Lexiphanes*, to satirize contemporaries for their far-fetched or un-Attic
Atticisms, imbedded in a jumble of solecisms.

An adequate idea of his style and qualities
as a writer must be obtained by actual reading
of selections from his best works, such as the
Charon, Cock, Fisher, Icaromenippus, the *True
Story, Marine Dialogues*, the *Dialogues of the*

Gods, and the *Dialogues of the Dead,* but the
sparkling wit of his satire, at a first reading,
constantly deflects the reader from consciousness that his reason is being led captive. Undisguised impossibilities become possible, rational, actual through Lucian's method of
solemnly confirming the " utterly impossible "
by specifying details. When, for example,
chanticleer before dawn addresses his owner
in human speech, the shoemaker is given no
chance to recover from that surprise before he
is swept on by the still greater surprise of find-
ing that his cock is Pythagoras and this fact is,
in turn, made inescapable by the unimpeachable autobiography forthwith detailed by the
temporary rooster. Or, again, if we have a
sinking feeling at the pit of our reason, as
the Birdman flies up to heaven on his wings,
(one an eagle's, and one a vulture's) we lose
the sensation by the time we have put in for
repairs at the private garage of Empedocles
on the Moon, and, when once we are seated,
en famille, at table with the Olympians, all the
household economics of the gods seem a mere
matter of course.

Through it all Lucian is arguing without
deflecting our attention. That is a surprise

only realized when he pauses to inject some
longer, more undisguised screed. This momentum that carries us along is generated by his
esprit and his power of imagination — his
" fantaisie spirituelle " — the two outstanding
qualities of his style. This " esprit " is as difficult to diagnose as is charm in a woman. The
particular features of the subject in hand may
be beautiful or ugly, bizarre or matter-of-fact,
but his charm, his verve still dominates. Lucian is master, *par excellence,* of an irony now
biting, now subtly malicious, now good-humoured and sympathetic. When he steps down
from his proper rôle as artist and gives way to
personal polemic, this subtler irony is liable
to degenerate into bitterness imperfectly sea-
soned with Attic salt.

The Satiric Dialogues, naturally, best reflect
Lucian's dramatic art which was influenced by
certain favourite dialogues of Plato and is often
redolent of Aristophanic humour. To speak of
imitation is beside the point. He borrows from
both with each hand. But his debts are entered on an open ledger and the borrowed
capital has been put out at interest. No Greek,
for example, could fail to be reminded of Try-
gaeus and his journey to heaven on the beetle,

in the *Peace* of Aristophanes, by the aerial exploit of Icaromenippus but Lucian's new occasion gives him opportunity for new and original effects.

In narration Lucian's force and grace are on a par with his dramatic skill in the dialogues. He seizes upon the salient point, reënforces it by unexpected detail, and carries us, easily acquiescent, into another impossibility. The *True Story*, the best known of his narrations and for centuries a quarry for imitators, still retains its primacy over all comers.

Even experts in the art of writing may gather fresh suggestion from a study of Lucian's methods. The diagnosis of the styles of Voltaire and Lucian, made with wonted Gallic precision by M. Croiset, is both a stimulating comparative study in the artistry of writing and a skilful indication of Lucian's assets and limitations. To a Frenchman, himself possessed of a perfect instrument of expression, the sympathetic understanding of both writers was possible, and no one except a Frenchman could, with so good a grace, attribute to Lucian preëminence, in certain particulars, over Voltaire's mastery in language.

V. PHILOSOPHY AND ETHICS

IN LUCIAN'S scheme of life we need spend less time, than we must in the case of the Platonized Socrates, in distinguishing the purely speculative from the practical. Although he speaks so often and so glibly of philosophy and the philosophers he does not concern himself in detail with transmuting the transcendental into the pragmatic. He does, on occasion, contemptuously record certain obvious catch-words and theses from the pre-Socratic philosophers, from Socrates himself and his contemporaries, or from the subsequent realignment and development of philosophic speculation, but all this affords him mere copy for his cartoons or, at best, an abridged manual of practical rules of conduct. Usually he remained not only tone-deaf to the Pythagorean " music of the spheres " but apparently stone-blind to Plato's " vision of the more excellent in the ideal." Only rarely does he allow some deeper misgiving to break through the salt crust of satire, as in his allusion to the haven of true philosophy, subtly reminiscent of a beautiful passage in Plato's *Republic*. One early piece, indeed, the *Nigrinus,* in form a short letter introducing a dialogue, gives us his contact with a philosopher of the nobler type that he seldom recognizes as existing. This piece reads like the record of a " conversion " from the vain desires of this world to a higher life. Although this early dream " fades into the light of common day " in Lucian's subsequent bitterness and satire upon charlatans, it is only fair to remember that he began his career with this underlying ideal.

If we close our minds to the brilliant artistry of his dialogues we may apprehend his superficial attitude towards pure philosophy and science and, at the same time, appraise at its face value his avowed ethical purpose — his crusade against shams.

In this crusade, as was natural, contemporary creeds and practices were chiefly his concern. In his *Sale of Soul Samples* only two pre-Socratics are put up at auction. Pythagoras was a show-piece, suitable to start the bidding. Lucian treats with amused inadequacy his esoteric doctrines of " reminiscence," the diapason of the planets and all the intricacies of the

great master's mathematical imagination. The
Pythagoras proxy is made to say:

> PYTH. I will teach you how to count.
> BUYER. But I know how already.
> PYTH. How do you count?
> BUYER. One, two, three, four.
> PYTH. See? What you think " four " is " ten "
> and a perfect triangle and the oath we swear by.
> BUYER. Now, by your greatest oath, Number
> Four, never did I hear propositions more divine
> nor more sacrosanct!

Next, the " four elements " are anachronisti-
cally attributed to Pythagoras, and Lucian
then passes on to ridicule the doctrine of immortality and the transmigration of souls. Next
come dietary data and other stock jokes — the
Pythagorean five years' silence, embryo of the
Trappist's vow; abstention from eating beans
(with hard-boiled reasons); and, finally, the
traditional golden thigh of the master. This
particular Pythagorean talent was not wrapped
inactive in a napkin, for we find that later,[16]
in the " Islands of the Blest," the whole right
side of the philosopher has aurified. Here the
sagacious bidder buys him promptly, as an in-
vestment, for one hundred and eighty dollars.

Lucian, careless of chronology, does not put
up another pre-Socratic philosopher until he

has disposed of two later ones. There is good and sufficient artistic reason for this order. Heracleitus the Obscure, the pessimist, is saved up to pair with Democritus the Optimist — a stock contrast. They both prove unsalable. Lucian betrays little appreciation of the significance of either of them. Heracleitus's *aeon,* to be sure, is neatly played with, but the Atomic theory of Democritus, adumbration of the modern *ion,* is dismissed with a punning joke. Lucian elsewhere [17] recognizes this theory as part of the Epicurean eclecticism and, with his characteristic trick of being specific, identifies their special brand of atoms. The " Birdman," appraising from his airy height the relative insignificance of earth's broad acres, sees that the largest landholder is " farming an estate no bigger than an Epicurean atom." Plato himself, it may be remembered, had ignored Democritus and, anyhow, it would be owlish literalness to expect the satirist to spoil his burlesque by telling all that he knows. Even in the serious *apologia* of the sequel, *The Fisher,* Lucian, when he attempts to restore the philosophers to their rightful perspective, as contrasted with the charlatans masquerading in their cloaks, emphasizes only their ethical value

[50]

and their contributions to literary art. He leaves the real factor in the personal equation unsolved and an unknown quantity. In this sequel Heracleitus is altogether ignored and Pythagoras, referred to repeatedly, maintains his orthodox silence, though his greedy followers urge his date as reason for precedence — " first come, first served."

After disposing of the costly Pythagoras antique, the auctioneer next puts up Diogenes the Cynic. This Great Unwashed, domiciled in a Corinthian *jar* — (not a " tub," that curiously wooden mistranslation!) — was still, after more than four centuries, available as a sample of contemporary exponents of the strenuous life. Although Lucian, on occasion, was wont to masquerade under the incognito of Menippus, he became "exceeding mad " against the charlatan Cynics of his own day whom he thinks of as so many " soap-box " radicals, fanatics or hypocrites.

The treatment of Diogenes is purely pragmatic and external. The Cynic explains to an intending buyer how a systematic course in trampling upon all the conventionalities of life, ignoring all comforts, and welcoming discomfort and pain, will equip one to be a guide of others: " You'll need no culture, nor dialectics, nor nonsense. It will be a short cut to fame if you merely have shamelessness and impudence and learn thoroughly how to play the black-guard." (Some of this has, incidentally, a modern sound!) Hermes, the auctioneer, gladly accepts a " marked down " price of six cents. This added insult to Diogenes is still rankling when he is put forward, in the sequel, as the most available prosecuting attorney. Was this Lucian's relative valuation of the philosophy of the Cynics at this period? He does not deign to give any inkling of their real doctrine, although their rejection of polytheism may easily have appealed to him.

Next Aristippus of Cyrene is put up for sale. He made pleasure the *summum bonum,* drawing from the common master, Socrates, this one distortion of his teaching just as the " Dog-philosophers " had gone off with only one bare bone of the Socratic anatomy. Aristippus, however, is too drunk to speak up for himself and this " professor of luxury " and " experienced chef " remains unsold. Later on, Epicurus himself is successfully auctioned off as a more adequate representative of this philosophy of life. In the sequel, however, both of them quickly

give out, through weariness of their pampered
flesh, when the Resurrected Philosophers are
in hot pursuit of their calumniator. Thus Lucian could include in his satire the vulnerable
features of Epicurean practice, though, on occasion, he praised, almost as if a disciple, the
nobler creed of Epicurus himself.

After the unsuccessful attempt, above noticed, to sell off the out-of-date Heracleitus
and the unpractical Democritus, Socrates is
put up for sale. It might be expected that he,
at least, as an exponent of the ethical, would
escape calumny; but Lucian outdoes Aristophanes himself with one wicked thrust. In the
sequel, however, he makes clear enough that
he is merely unmasking the license lurking beneath contemporary cloaks. His mockery of
Socrates otherwise, as, for example, his queer
oaths, is good humoured enough and he does
not, in this dialogue, even attack his belief in
immortality which was for Lucian an irritating
dogma. Elsewhere,[18] indeed, in a confidential
family talk between the dog-janitor and the
dog-philosopher Menippus, Cerberus declares
that Socrates, at his death, merely put on a
brave front to impress those who were present.
"But," continues Cerberus, "when he peeped

down into the chasm, and the darkness became visible, and I, giving him a hemlock-bite as he was still holding back, jerked him down by the foot, he howled like an infant and bewailed his own children and ' turned every which way.' ''

In this " Sale," however, the buyer next asks Socrates about his mode of life. He replies that he lives in a *Republic* of his own and goes in for his own *Laws*. Suddenly we are dealing with Plato himself. The buyer demands a sample of these laws and there is served up to him forthwith a choice digest of the matrimonial communism in Book V of *The Republic* of Plato. Next the buyer demands the sum and substance of his system. The Socrates-Plato explains:

S.P. The Ideas and Exemplars of what is really existent. For you must know that of whatsoever you behold — the earth, things on the earth, the heavens, the sea — of all these, unseen images stand outside the universe.

BUYER. Stand? Where?

S.P. Nowhere. For if they were anywhere, they would not exist.

BUYER. I do not see these Exemplars of which you speak.

S.P. Naturally. For you are blind in your soul's eye.

Finally the customer purchases the Platonized Socrates for two talents — more than two thousand dollars — for the lot, or, for each one more than the sum total paid in for all the other soul-samples, who together net only $810.06. It is as if Lucian in the midst of his raillery would indicate his relative estimate of Socrates — too secure in his noble fame to be harmed by ribald innuendo — and of Plato, whose primacy he is constrained to acknowledge, on more than one occasion.

Now comes the hasty sale, for thirty-six dollars, of a real Epicurean. The comments though not very vicious, certainly do not suggest that Lucian, at the moment, was an orthodox Epicurean.

Then the Stoic, Lucian's *bête noir,* is put through the third degree with great gusto. Catch-words from the Stoic vocabulary are ridiculed. The Rt. Reverend Syllogism is brought out. Chrysippus — presumably it is he, his busts were omnipresent [19] — cites solemnly sundry stock conundrums and proves that it is more altruistic, and therefore more blessèd, to receive than to give. Systematic logic is satirized by his triumphant propounding of illogical syllogisms, with undistributed middles. He is bought for two hundred and sixteen dollars by a large syndicate, a detail which reflects the numerical popularity of the Court creed.

Then the Peripatetic is sold for three hundred and sixty dollars, the largest sum received for any lot offered except the Socrates-Plato. Lucian refrains, very noticeably, from any violent thrust at Aristotle. There is, of course, good-humoured bantering of the one " who knows all and sundry"; the one " who can tell how deep the sunshine penetrates the sea "; who knows " of what sort is the soul-life of the oyster "; or of his X-ray insight into the formation of the embryo, etc. The solid nucleus of biological investigation, Aristotle's most permanent contribution to science, was as uninspiring to sophistic rhetoricians as had been, indeed, to the ethical preoccupation of Socrates the pregnant theories of Anaxagoras. And Lucian, although he must have his joke about the " double " Aristotle, the exoteric and the esoteric, is constrained to honour his three peculiarly Hellenic qualities, " moderation, seemliness, and harmony of life," and to comment on the triple *summum bonum* inherent in the soul (or mind), the body, and the environment. As far as his own treatment was concerned, Aristotle need not have come up from Hades along with the other resurgent protestants to demand satisfaction.

Finally, a Sceptic is sold for one Attic mina, about eighteen dollars, a trifling price for an able-bodied slave. He is addressed as Pyrrhias, "carrots," to suggest at once a red-headed slave and also the name of the founder of the school, Pyrrho, a contemporary of Aristotle who, as contrasted with the Stoics, developed this tendency of the Academics. Lucian is, on various occasions, prone to merge the Sceptics and Academics together. Zeus, for example, seated over the trapdoor for ascending prayers, in the *Icaromenippus,* when he has the chance to make an equally good thing out of two identical promissory offerings in two mutually exclusive prayers, has that "usual *Academic* experience and, like Pyrrho, remained on the fence."

It is a little surprising that Lucian, the cavilling agnostic, who might be expected to sympathize with the Sceptic philosophy, treats it as contemptuously as he treated Plato's unreal " realities " or as he would treat today the incorporealities of Christian " Science." Pyrrhias, when asked what practical service he is good for, describes himself as a general utility man who can do anything and everything " except catch a runaway slave." As reason for this handicap he explains that he cannot " catch on " since there is no *tangible* standard for anything!

It is difficult, in fact, to identify Lucian with any school. If, as is sometimes assumed, the allusion [20] to himself as a "high-priced sophist " means that he actually held " in days gone by," out in Gaul, an imperial " professorship," it cannot have been while he was coquetting with the Cynics who, like the Sceptics, were ineligible for imperial preferment. We learn, for example, from the somewhat clinical testing of a candidate in the *Eunuchus* (where, indeed, it was not a question of sect but of sex) that only the conventional " Big Four " — Academics, Epicureans, Peripatetics, and Stoics, summarized by Gildersleeve as the " Established Church " in contrast with " Dissenters " like the Cynics — were eligible for these large imperial stipends. Lucian certainly was not a Stoic; hardly an Epicurean at this date; nor was he equipped, as it would seem, to elucidate the doctrines of either of the other two schools.

In this *Sale of Soul Samples* he has held up to ridicule, in varying degree, all the four officially recognized schools as well as the Cynics and Sceptics. Pythagoras, Heracleitus and Democritus were also " good copy." Empedocles, one of his pet aversions, was well toasted in Aetna, warmed over in the Moon,[21] and will appear in the sequel in a very hot temper.

An appraisal of the companion-piece or sequel, *The Fisher*, would be a study of Lucian's best qualities, as a stylist, in the dramatic dialogue. It is consciously Aristophanic in the opening scene where the " Resurgents," on furlough from Hades for one day — the same device as is used in the *Charon* — enter, in hot pursuit of their alleged calumniator. There is a succession of dramatic scenes. Lucian with difficulty escapes lynching and persuades his captors that they must, by virtue of their own love of justice, grant him a judicial trial.

With much reluctance on the part of the philosophers, this is conceded and the defendant easily proves his real innocence. All the censure and ridicule that he had poured out in the " Sale " was entirely directed against the charlatans of his own day. His triumphant, unanimous acquittal is a matter of course. The next thing is to punish the pseudo-philosophers. He receives his high commission from Lady Philosophy herself — to go up and down the world branding the false and crowning the genuine. The last scene, which suggested the title, contains skilful satire. He borrows a hook and line, dedicated in the Parthenon by a grateful fisherman, borrows also from the Priestess some gold as bait, and proceeds to fish over the side of the Acropolis for the greedy dog-fish and other sharks who swarm in these second-century waters. By his selection of a representative catch, he again betrays his intellectual indifference towards the schools that were not continued as a contemporary living issue — he was not after stale fish. In fact, he lands sample fish from four only of the six main schools: a dog-shark for the Cynics, but no Sceptic — probably they could not " catch on " — and specimen fish from the Platonic, Peripatetic and Stoic shoals, but no sluggish Epicurean! The fish are biting well, but he fears that he will lose his gold bait. These samples suffice. From them Lucian can feed the multitude, his hearers.

Various other works of Lucian must be read for a full understanding of his attitude towards philosophy and ethics. Brief suggestion only of three more can be given here. All of these differ from each other in content.

The *Hireling Philosophers*, one of Lucian's most amusing pieces, vivid, witty, bitter, is a warning, in letter form though without super-scription, to a friend, against selling his liberty and his intellect to lend éclat to a rich patron. With unsparing detail he pictures the life led by a domesticated scholar whether in the great city establishment or *en route* for the country-place in the servants' carriage, sandwiched between a vulgar valet and the mistress's " beauty-expert," where, incidentally, he is compelled to give maieutic assistance to my lady's Maltese lapdog which has been confided to his especial care. This tragic, though amus-ing, recital has been a warning to many an impecunious scholar.[22] Lucian himself in his old age, when dependent on a government salary, feels it incumbent upon him to defend himself from his own satire by writing a feeble *Apologia*.

The *Symposium*, like the *Eunuchus*, shows us Lucian in his most unrestrained humour in his satire upon contemporary philosophers. And yet, outrageous as it is, only for a few

sentences does it degenerate into the banality
of bitterness that sometimes mars his pages.
In this piece he gathers together at a wedding-
feast representatives of the four great sects
(with *two* Stoics for good measure) and other
prominent persons. Later a Cynic enters un-
invited not as a mere entrée but as the *pièce
de résistance*. In a succession of rapid scenes
Lucian gives us the most incredible situations, filled with jealousy and lust, wrangling,
vituperation, gouged-out eyes, truncated noses,
blows and blood. But it is incomparable for
skill in narration and dramatic suggestion.

The *Hermotimus or the Sects* was written
when Lucian was forty years old, when he is
consciously turning to his proper business of
literary creation. It is his longest and, in some
respects, his most interesting work although
not to be classed with his best dramatic and
artistic productions. It is his serious deliver-
ance on philosophy or, more strictly, upon the
systems of ethics. In form it is an undisguised
reflection of Plato's dialogues. It was doubtless
intended by Lucian to be his *magnum opus* and
yet, in a sense, it is his most conspicuous failure. Attempting serious dialogue, he either lectures or answers himself back in falsetto like a

marionette-exhibitor. We might be tempted, at times, to say the same of the Platonized-Socrates, but the *Republic* of Plato is constructive; it rears a lofty dwelling-place not made with hands, whereas Lucian uproots the very foundations. It is his " Confession of Unfaith." The pupil Hermotimus, who has been painfully working the stony tract of Stoicism these forty years — he is now sixty — is relentlessly driven from one refuge to another until, with his hopes shattered, he gives in at the last and exclaims in effect like Faust:

> *Naught can we know with certainty —*
> *That sears the very heart in me!*

It is not simply the Stoics that have been weighed and found wanting. They are merely one outstanding illustration. " Lycinus " assures the now disenchanted Hermotimus that it is the same with all creeds — neither Jew nor Gentile, Stoic churchman nor Cynic dissenter can guide you up the hill of Virtue. His substitute creed is " Common Sense and scepticism." " Keep sober," he says with Epicharmus, " Keep sober and remember to doubt."

We may well be sceptical as to how much Lucian actually accomplished for the ethics of his own generation; some critics consider his avowed crusade against shams as rhetorical arrogance; others, inclined to grant, even to great men, a more generous margin of self-deception, may believe that Lucian, in his own estimate of his rôle, was really an honest Commissioner for repairing the highways and byways of his time.

VI. THE SUPERNATURAL

1. THE GODS

LUCIAN'S Crusade against Shams, however much or little reasoned conviction we may be disposed to concede to him, was not confined to attacks upon the unethical practices of contemporaries who posed as philosophers. His satire, now bald and bitter, now glowing with iridescent charm, pursued relentlessly all superstitions and manifestations of a belief in the supernatural. The most intransigent scientists of the middle of the nineteenth century in their consecrated quest for protoplasm were hardly more bitter than he against all belief in " things unseen." They, to be sure, were "sustained by an unfaltering trust " in their constructive aims, whereas Lucian was cynically destructive, an iconoclast who could set up in the vacated shrines " no good God except good Greek." [23] A continuous trip with him through the devastated region of his No-gods' land would become depressing were it not for his unfailing humour that acts as a partial counter-irritant against pessimism.

To illustrate fully his hostility to the old established Greek religion and to current superstitions, we should have to lay under contribution ten or twelve, at least, of his best pieces
and add, moreover, many of the fifty-six short
Dialogues of the Gods and *Dialogues of the
Dead*.

Experts on the novel point out that the number of really distinct plots is, in the nature of
things, very limited. Lucian's writings contain
a disconcerting number of repetitions, both of
ideas and matter. He was not by way of writing an orderly Manual of Ethics! When he
wrote his " sequels," they were evidently intended for audiences previously addressed, but,
as a rule, he could safely count either upon
new hearers or upon his own adroitness and
wit in presenting shop-worn rôles under a new
mask.

As to his inconsistencies, these are not of a
character to indicate either moral obliquity or
lack of stability. The most striking apparent
inconsistency is his shift to vitriolic vituperation of the Cynics after his earlier cordial, and
even partisan, approval of their creed. The or-
dinary explanation is, doubtless, the correct
one. His frank adherence to the Cynic Menip-

pus as a model continued into a part, at least, of his best period. When it came to personal satire, as in the case of the suicide Peregrinus, he was under no bonds to any creed. It does not seem practicable to use this criterion with exactitude, in establishing the chronological sequence of his writings.

Minor inconsistencies are, of course, deliberate artistic devices. Such, for example, is the insouciance of his whim of the moment when Charon, at one time, conducts his ferry-boat on the "pay-as-you-enter" system and refuses embarcation to a would-be passenger who cannot pay down his obol, and rejects the suggested compromise of allowing him to work out his fare, while, in another dialogue, he willingly permits a stow-away to work his passage by baling bilge-water or by taking a hand at the oar. Quite different from such deliberate devices is the possible moral deterioration of Lucian grown old and submitting to imperial patronage. To those who seek an ethical lesson this may suggest that a philosophy of negation is no safe sheet-anchor.

In his *Zeus Cross-questioned* he relentlessly annihilates the sovereignty of the gods. "Cyniscus" (a Menippean incognito) is allowed by the Chairman of the gods to ask one thing, after promising that he will not ask for wealth or power. He therefore propounds the leading question: " Do Destiny and the Fates really dispose of all things without appeal? " Zeus, falling into the trap, goes the limit in emphasizing, as a cardinal doctrine for all orthodox belief, that the ultimate decision for gods as well as for men, rests with the Fates. The logical application is easy for the Cynic. On this basis the inequalities of life cannot be relieved by any divine intervention, and the suggestion of any readjustment by rewards and punishments after death is seen to be preposterous. This age-old contradiction between predestination and free-will is, of course, a favourite weapon with Lucian. He uses it most artistically, perhaps, in one of the *Dialogues of the Dead,* where Minos, the judge, has already passed judgment on a certain tyrant and then, out of deference to the legal right of the defendant to show cause why sentence should not be passed upon him, makes the mistake of allowing the condemned criminal to interpellate the court. Minos has an irreproachably judicial mind and is led to admit that an executioner, for example, is no more responsible for carrying out " orders from above " than is the sword itself with which he beheads the criminal. Sostratus, the tyrant, therefore claims, and receives, from the logical judge the cancellation of his sentence. " But," says Minos, " see to it that you don't put up the rest of the corpses to asking similar questions!"

The *Tragical Zeus* is an elaboration of the foregoing. Zeus appears, this time in the bosom of the family, voicing the tragic crisis in which he finds himself by declaiming adaptations from Euripides, with some Homer thrown in. In answer to anxious metrical questions from his children and caustic free-prose remarks from his wife—(" *I* haven't," she says, " swallowed Euripides whole ") — he reveals how he, disguised as a philosopher, has been listening to a most atheistic attack made by a certain Epicurean — (Lucian's proxy here) — with only very feeble rebuttal from a Stoic philosopher. After some discussion of ways and means, Hermes, in canonical hexameters, calls a panoecumenical council of the gods. Not even a nymph fails to heed the summons. An insoluble difficulty develops at once as to the question of seating the delegates. There are all grades of blue blood and new blood, from the

Twelve Olympians down through half-gods to foreigners of outside pedigree. More perplexing still is the case of accredited statues, involving the question of size, material, and the value of artistic workmanship. If the foreign gold gods are to have front seats then the marble Cnidian Aphrodite, though one of " The Twelve " and of Praxitelean workmanship, is relegated to the rear — and yet, as she justly urges, Homer had, in so many words, called her " golden Aphrodite." Finally, the Colossus of Rhodes, though made of bronze, urges that by mere tonnage displacement he is worth more than many gold statuettes. Zeus realizes that the Colossus in front would take up too much space, no matter if they " sit close," and would, moreover, obstruct the view of a whole wedge of gods behind him. He is told to stand up in the rear. The question of precedence stands over for a future session.

Zeus now puts before the gods the crisis that is upon them — how contemporary atheistic tendencies are to be met. To win the attention of this more exoteric audience and warned, perhaps, by his wife's sarcasm, he drops tragedy and takes to Demosthenes. But even his Demosthenes soon gives out and he rehearses —

probably in the contemporary *lingua franca* of the Common Greek — the depressing incident of yesterday, and asks for suggestions. Momus, the official Censor — one of Lucian's numerous proxies — speaks first and makes matters worse. Poseidon then makes the practical suggestion that Zeus should take executive action and with his thunderbolt put Damis the Epicurean *hors de combat* before he can finish his atheistic attack. Zeus, with some irritation, reminds him that only the Fates could authorize the death of Damis. Moreover his death would leave the question itself unsettled. Apollo then suggests that Timocles the Stoic, god-fearing as he may be, is hardly the person to entrust with the gods' very existence, which is now upon the razor's edge. They should appoint a clear-voiced coadjutor. This gives the Momus-Lucian the chance for a double thrust at the Stoics and at the involved oracles of Apollo. He urges Apollo himself to foretell which one will win out in tomorrow's debate. Apollo replies that he can't give a proper oracle, away from his dark-room and his medium at Delphi. None the less he does give, under pressure, an eight-line hexameter oracle which, to say the least, is non-committal. Forcible intervention is again suggested by the strenuous Heracles but he too, like Poseidon, is sharply reminded by Zeus that such action lies on the knees, not of the gods, but of the Fates. A vicious Lucianic twist is given by Zeus's careful explanation that Heracles, while alive on earth as a free-will agent, might perhaps have performed his "twelve labours" but now that he is a mere emeritus god he is no longer able to initiate anything.

At this juncture there arrives from Athens an ectoplasmic Hermes-of-the-Marketplace, the rhetorician Hermagoras, a *pro tem,* liaison god, to say that the debate is again in full swing. There is nothing for it but to stoop over, listen and hope for the best. Zeus sharply orders the Hours to unbar the Olympian front-door and to remove all intervening clouds so as to secure an unimpeded view and hearing of the debate below.

This paves the way, artistically, for a dialogue within the dialogue, a device used elsewhere by Lucian — most happily, perhaps, in the *Charon.* The Stoic champion of the gods — arguments, syllogisms, illustrations and all — is of course overwhelmed but, though defeated, he has the courage of his earlier conviction and, not being a mere denatured god, pursues his successful opponent with a shower of missiles, giving Hermes the cue for some final words of comfort to his depressed father, selected not from tragedy but this time from Menander's comedy: *Never say die!* "You've suffered nothing evil, if nothing you admit." [24]

In the *Called Assembly of Gods* it would seem that Lucian had followed up Zeus's promise, made above, to settle questions of precedence and, still more pressing, of divine eligibility. Hermes proclaims the opportunity for free discussion as to full-breed gods. The question of the eligibility of resident-aliens and half-breeds is up for consideration.

Momus is, of course, the first to gain recognition by the presiding officer, Zeus. He proceeds at once to criticize the pedigrees of Dionysus, Pan, *et al.* Zeus warns him not to say a word about Asclepius or Heracles. Momus then takes up certain ugly reports about Zeus himself — his promiscuous birth-places, metamorphoses and even burial-places. Zeus makes no rebuttal except to warn him against any reference to Ganymede. Momus switches off to a catalogue of queer Oriental and Egyptian gods—some of them cannot even speak Greek! He comes around, naturally, to the growing

menace of the worship of the goddess "Chance,"
which is upsetting the stock-market of sacrifices. Finally, he proposed an elaborate bill,
worded in good Athenian form. This is, in
brief: Whereas numerous and sundry unnatu-
ralized and polyglot gods have slipped into the
registry without establishing title or even paying the fee, and whereas the over-populating of
heaven has so curtailed the supply of ambrosia
and nectar that the latter now costs eighteen
dollars the half-pint, be it resolved: That a
Commission be appointed consisting of seven
full-breed gods, three of the old Cronus council and four, including the chairman, from
"The Twelve," fully empowered to enroll such
gods as are proved genuine and to send back to
their ancestral tombs and barrows all half-
breeds and foreigners. Penalty for non-observ-
ance of the Commission's findings: To be
thrown into Tartarus. Incidentally, everybody
is to keep to his or her own specialty. Athena,
for example, is not to practice medicine; Asclepius is not to give oracles; Apollo is to cut
down his overlapping activities. The philosophers are to be warned and the statues of all
illegitimate gods are to be taken down and
replaced by images of Zeus, Hera, Apollo, etc.

Zeus, not daring to put the decree to vote in this mixed assembly, arbitrarily announces it as " carried!"

To include here, by way of illustration, extracts from the twenty-six *Dialogues of the Gods* would shift the emphasis from their more important quality as artistic, dramatic pictures. But the satire in them, though veiled, is the more effective because the gods convict themselves of folly and passion. They plead guilty by explaining. Zeus and the others come before us in all their chryselephantine pomp, but they lay open their breasts to us with confiding frankness and show their unlovely and wooden interiors. Such testimony admits no rebuttal. The case goes against them by default.

The thirty *Dialogues of the Dead* transfer Lucian's frontal attack upon the gods and an overruling Providence to a campaign against the superstitions encrusted upon the belief in a life after death.[25] The juxtaposition of things material and immaterial gives Lucian's fancy a welcome opportunity. Men and gods, earth and heaven reappear reflected in the mirror of the Infernal Lake like a landscape inverted in the water, while the shore's edge, dividing the real and the unreal, shrinks to a mathematical

[75]

line. Charon's boat glides over the unruffled water. It, or its reflected image, will surely make port. The certainty of "death and taxes" is exemplified in the person of the Collector Aeacus checking off the way-bill.

By the very virulence of his satire on "corpse-affairs" Lucian almost seems to betray a lurking misgiving that there may be a sequel to this life. If so, however, it was an unconscious betrayal. He was consistent in his nonchalant attitude towards a belief in immortality: now amused, as in his inimitable creation of the Chanticleer-avatar of Pythagoras; now pungently contemptuous at the sight of a pickled mummy; now rollickingly logical, as when Heracles in Hades carefully explains that his immortal half is honeymooning in Heaven; or, finally, pityingly patronizing towards the misguided worshippers of "the crucified sophist" who have persuaded themselves that they are to live on through time unending.[26]

His own insistence on the *liberté et égalité et fraternité* in Hades, as an antidote to the inequalities of riches and poverty in this life, forces him, as though with an effort, to portray their real unreality. The actors in these brief dramas are not clothed upon with unnecessary rhetoric, but the snub-nosed skulls still have "speculation in their eyes," the white femora step out bravely, and the vacant ribs reëcho the Cynic's ventriloquism.

Life's futility is presented from various sides. We learn the vanity of riches that yield the Ferryman's fee as their only dividend; we see the frustrated legacy-hunters; see, too, beauty and kisses, flow of rhetoric and flowing beard of the philosophers, pedigree and patrimony, the fair fame of Socrates — all alike — go by the board and drift astern in the boat's livid wake as the passengers prepare to step ashore with naked bones that need fear no nip of Cerberus. Or, the fancy changes and the dead arrive before the judge still branded with the stigmata of sins for which they are to suffer, *in propria persona,* most humanly as they deserve.

"*Crossing the Bar*" [27] or *The Tyrant* is a much larger canvas, painted in more lurid colours, but on the same gray and livid background.

The Subway officials, the crew and the passengers on Charon's crowded boat are painted in with swift impressionism. Atropos "with

the abhorréd shears " has " slit the thin-spun
life " of 1004 persons today. Aeacus, the Rev-
enue Inspector at the Ferry, finds the shipment
one corpse short as per Bill of Lading. The
flurried Corpse-conductor, Hermes, with the
aid of the now jovial Cynic, retrieves the Tyrant who has nearly made good his escape up
the funicular tunnel. This unprecedented delay
to the cable-line of the Fates, usually running
on schedule time, angers the Ferryman, who
has already lost two trips. He hurries all on
board, except Micyllus,[28] the cobbler, who has
no obol to pay his fare, and casts loose his
mooring. The cobbler, long since eager for his
mansion on the ever-gray shore, is in despair
but, realizing that he cannot drown since he is
dead already, plunges into the Salt Lake whose
high specific gravity easily buoys up his now
negligible weight. Being in the swim he even
offers to race Charon to the landing. This,
however, is not *de rigeur*. Clotho, the senior
Spinster, sailing as special supercargo, salvages
the unconventional corpse and, for lack of other
accommodations, gives him an upper bunk on
the shoulders of the Tyrant. The scene, where
Rhadamanthus pronounces judgment, informs
us that all previous sins leave stigmata on the

sinner's body. Under microscopic examination the Cynic is found to have many faint traces of former sins. His strenuous philosophic virtue, however, has entirely obliterated his guilt and he is passed without conditions. The cobbler, whose poverty is apparently counted unto him as righteousness, has a skin as smooth as a baby's and he is at once billed through to the Islands of the Blest. But Megapenthes, the multimillionaire tyrant, is in a parlous state — livid all over with confluent stigmata. His lamp and couch, summoned as eyewitnesses, give illuminating and bed-rock testimony. For such an imperial sinner a special punishment is devised. He is not allowed to drink of the water of Lethe, the River of Oblivion. His " sorrow's crown of sorrows " shall be the eternal and undimmed recollection of his former life of luxury. For him we may delimit " Hades " and translate the title as *The Hell-bent Voyage.*

Two other pieces, the *Menippus* and the *Icaromenippus* are pertinent here and also suggest how Lucian developed his own negatives. Their inverted mechanism is identical — the preambles; the miraculous trips to Hades and Heaven respectively; the Synod of Corpses and the Council of Olympians; the inferences drawn; and even the simplicity of the two short-cuts back to Earth are pendants of each other. In each of them a comedy of Aristophanes — the *Frogs* and the *Peace* — furnishes a happy suggestion. The main difference lies in the relative degree of finish. The *Menippus or Necromancy* is apparently a mere charcoal sketch, or a snap-shot caught by the help of Persephone's flashlight, of shadows of shades, whereas in the *Icaromenippus* the artist, working *en plein air,* paints at leisure his finished picture with perfected technique and unfading colours.

This latter is an elaborate satire on Greek religion, in Lucian's most brilliant vein, prefaced by a somewhat detailed and irritable analysis of the net yield of philosophic speculation and physical investigation, as Lucian chose to appraise them. The transcendental Birdman, with the synthetic name, Icaromenippus, explains why he found it necessary to obtain, by a visit to Heaven [29] itself, first hand information in the hope of coördinating conflicting statements of contemporary philosophers. This original purpose is not ignored in the end but is merged in the larger question

[80]

of man's relation to the gods. This question of universal import is asked today. No more deadly comment has ever been made on the immoral futility of the necessarily conflicting petitions raised by embattled nations, each to its Tribal God, than Lucian's witty résumé of Zeus's daily office-business.

Daedalus, incidentally the father of flying as well as of other far more important contributions to progress, had fastened on with wax his own and his son's wings, a device adapted only to a low-altitude flight across the Aegean. Icarus soared high and was lost. Icaromenippus, however, provides against this by a greatly improved method of attaching his wings — one an eagle's, one a vulture's. This combination, indeed, of the celestial and the terrestrial nearly wrecked the venture. Hampered by the inferior vulture's wing, he puts in for repairs at the Lunar garage conducted by Empedocles, an émigré from Aetna, in whose crater he had acquired mechanical skill by watching the Olympian blacksmith, Hephaestus, mending the points of the imperial thunderbolts, broken [30] on the rocks through Zeus's poor marksmanship. After various instructive episodes on the Moon, upward we fly forget-

ting, in the iridescent joys of the open road, all
earthly handicaps.

On the traveller's arrival at the front door
of the Imperial Palace, Hermes, the heavenly
" bell-hop," answers his knock and takes in his
name to Zeus. When admitted, he is thunder-
struck at the Father's loud voice and Titanic
glance but is secretly somewhat reassured by
observing that the gods are equally alarmed at
his own unexpected epiphany. But Zeus is con-
versant with Homer and the sacred rights of
guest-friendship, and before dinner takes his
guest for a walk to the most resonant part of
Heaven where the sound-waves concentrate
and bring up the prayers, day by day, through
window-like openings in the floors, covered by
lids. But Zeus was out for information also
and he asks: " What's the present quotation
on wheat in Greece? Was last winter very hard
on you? Do the vegetables need more rain? "
— and other questions including more personal
matters, such as the likelihood of the comple-
tion of his great Olympieium in Athens and
whether certain temple robbers have yet been
apprehended, and, finally and most important:
" What opinion do men have about me? " — a
question requiring some cleverness to answer

both respectfully and diplomatically. Zeus, in fact, reveals his own apprehension that the great extension of the elective system, with the consequent inclusion of so many deities in the curriculum, is resulting in a general indifference to all of them.

Arrived at the prayer-precinct, Zeus took off a lid and allowed his guest to bend over with him and hear the various requests, for example:

O Zeus, grant that I may become King! O Zeus, make my onions grow and my garlic! O Gods, grant that my father die soon!

And one and another would say:

Grant that I may fall heir to my wife's money! Grant me that I escape detection in plotting against my brother! God grant that I may win in my law-suit! Grant that I be crowned at the Olympic Games!

And of those who were sailing the seas, one prayed for the north wind to blow, another for the south wind. And the farmer asked for rain; the fuller for sunshine. Zeus, though carefully considering each request, did not grant them *all*. In fact, he was occasionally at a loss when diametrically opposite requests were accompanied by precisely equal offerings!

After the prayers, Zeus listened in at other trap-doors, designed for transmitting oracles or the names of those who were making sacrifices, and then gave out his orders for the day to the Winds and Seasons:

Today let it rain in Scythia! Let there be lightning among the Libyans! Let it snow in Greece! And: Northwind, do you blow in Lydia! and do *you*, Southwind, remain inactive! Let Westwind kick up the waves in the Adriatic! And let, we'll say, about fifteen hundred bushels of hail be scattered over Cappodocia!

The family dinner that follows gives Lucian abundant opportunity — and he seems never to miss a chance — for his cumulative satire. Although seated with the alien-resident gods of doubtful pedigree, Icaromenippus could see and hear everything. He even had the good-fortune to get a taste, on the sly, of the conventional nectar on which gods only may get drunk. The cup-bearer, Ganymede, out of sympathetic loyalty to his own human extraction, would come, whenever the attention of the gods was deflected, and pour out for the guest a half-pint or so of nectar. The food and drink were all of home production, furnished from the special preserves and cellars of various gods. Nor were the finer intellectual amusements — music, dancing and poetry — far to seek, the Muses, for example, singing selections from Hesiod's *Genesis of the Gods!*

Night came on somehow although Helios was present at the table, wearing his ever-blazing halo. A called assembly of the gods next morning repeats situations already familiar, but details differ and the humour seems new and alluring. On this occasion Zeus does not choose to admit that he is not master of Fate and he promises the excited gods that he will resort to the most drastic measures against all atheists — after the holidays! Just now it would be sacrilegious.

He gives specific directions for ridding themselves of their unusual guest: " Take off his wings so that he may never come here again " — (To construct *another* airship would doubtless have been treated as an infringement of Zeus's patent on the eagle!) — " and let Hermes take him down to the Earth today." " And the son of Cyllene," Icaromenippus concludes, " holding me suspended by my right ear " — (the seat of memory) — " brought me and set me down yesterday at eventide in the Potters' Quarter."

Lucian might have rested content with his

campaign against Zeus and his Olympians, on the one hand, and, on the other, against Pluto, the " nether Zeus," and his realm. His inspector Menippus had spied out all the weak points in Hades below and in Heaven above. The debâcle of the gods, supernal and infernal, was inevitable. But there still remained a third approach to the problem — the viewing of human life through divine binoculars. To effect this, Lucian presses into temporary service the god Hermes, the busy corpse-conductor, and the god Charon, another proxy for Lucian in place of the discarded Menippus. Although logically, along with the rest of the gods, these two also by Lucian's catholic satire should have lost their standing, they had, in fact, only taken on a new lease of life. Lucian's audiences were now, more than ever, on familiar speaking terms with them.

The *Charon* or *The Inspectors* is usually grouped with the *Dialogues of the Dead* and contains, indeed, many superficial points of contact with them. But its tone is different. Scathing satire and even harsh invective against tyrants are tempered by a finer humour and by more than a touch of pity for men dangling helplessly from the spindles of the

Fates. Not even in Lucian's bitter mind is
Death always a subject for ridicule. Its in-
evitableness seems to set free for once, a more
human sympathy lurking beneath his polished
cynicism. Comic actors do not necessarily
laugh behind their masks and, in reading the
Charon, we are even tempted to consider genuine an epigram, replete with feeling, that is
attributed to Lucian. It is on the death of a
child, named Callimachus:

> Me *unpitying Death has taken,*
> Me *a child of five years old,*
> Me *whose soul no grief has shaken —*
> S*mall time, true, my life had doled,*
> S*mall ills, too, my life did see,*
> We*ep not, therefore — not for me.*

Whether written by Lucian or no, this attitude
towards the death of the very young, while
delicate in its sympathy, is highly antiseptic
and not out of keeping with the nobler
" imperturbability " ($\dot{\alpha}\tau\alpha\rho\alpha\xi\dot{\iota}\alpha$) of Epicurus [31]
himself which was, perhaps, Lucian's best ideal.
Be that as it may, this dialogue, which in artistic conception and execution has few equals,
rises above Menippean cynicism. The " Inspectors," Charon and Hermes, meet on neutral

ground and the result of their review of human life is unexpectedly non-partisan. Charon, to be sure, newly arrived on a furlough from the Underworld, at the opening of the dialogue is convulsed with laughter at hearing a man eagerly accept a dinner invitation, only to be killed the next moment by a falling tile. This reminds him pleasantly of his ferry business and, indeed, before the end of the dialogue, he insists, out of purely professional curiosity, upon seeing the terrestrial cold-storage plants which serve as terminal depots for the shipping of his daily cargoes. But the illuminating discussion with Hermes concerning the panorama of human history unrolled before them culminates in an unconscious parallel to the altruism of the rich man in Hell's torment who is fain to have Lazarus, whilom beggar but now ensconced in Abraham's bosom, sent as a missionary to his surviving brothers to urge them to timely repentance. But, like the rich man's unselfish thought for the living, Charon's generous impulse to cry out and warn men of their folly is suppressed by Hermes with similar finality. The Fates are in control and men would not, and could not, " be persuaded, though one rose from the dead." We see, in

[88]

effect, the Fates floating above us. We see the
shadowy phantoms with which they mock us:
hopes, fears, ambitions, jealousy, wrath and
covetousness. Chilling, in spite of its comic
reminiscence, falls upon our ears the swift
résumé at the end: " Lord, what fools these
mortals be! Kings, golden ingots, funeral rites,
battles, but never a word about Charon! "

2. Applied Superstition

THE *Charon* makes a natural transition to
Lucian's crusades against contemporary applied superstition. Superstition did not die out
with the advent of Christianity. It is not dead
yet. The classic curtsy to Nemesis survives undisguised in our apologetic: " Knock on wood,"
and the very vigour of the well-groomed twentieth-century intellect seems to furnish surplus
energy for the rank fungus growth of Spiritism.

In this brilliant Age of the Antonines superstitions, home-made and oriental, flourished
under the genial sunlight of the Roman Empire alongside the noble philosophy inculcated
by Imperial example. Here also Lucian found
his opportunity for asserting his ethics of negation and also for covert or open attacks upon
contemporaries.

His *Lie-Fancier* [32] is a round-trip ticket for a journey through the bog-lands of the human mind, ancient and modern, guided by the self-lighting *ignes fatui* of the generations.

Tychiades, Lucian himself, pays a visit of condolence to a sufferer from gout. His advent momentarily interrupts, but does not dam up, a flood of supernatural incidents which are being exchanged between the sick man and a coterie of distinguished friends, including reverend heads of philosophic schools, among them a Platonic D.D., and the " scientific " family doctor. These authentic experiences include, first of all, sure cures for gouty feet. For example, the tooth of a field mouse, killed in a specific manner and picked up with the left hand and wrapped in the newly-skinned pelt of a lion or that of a female deer, still virgin, will stop the pain instanter. A dispute arose as to which skin is the more efficacious for a crippled foot. In the opinion of the majority the lion took the *pas,* so to say, because a lion is swifter than even a deer. Ten distinct miracles follow, giving Lucian his chance for his choicest art as a raconteur. Snakes and dragons are exorcised; a flying Hyperborean magician assists in a love-affair, calling up Hecate and

bringing the Moon down, and, finally, fetching
the by no means reluctant pretty-lady; a Syrian drives out a demon from one possessed —
the tenant departing " all black and smoke-
complexioned "; statues, accurately described,
take an active part in the family ménage; all
" Hell " and its contents gape open; the conventional ghost is laid; in a sick man's vision
the death of a neighbour is predicted, and immediately comes true; household implements
are metamorphosed by magic formulae into
efficient valets. Incidentally, two [33] of these
tales are securely embedded in European literature.

When the interchange of experiences touches
upon oracles the doubting Tychiades withdraws
from the séance. It may be significant that the
Tychiades-Lucian, while defending his scepticism, rejects the inference that he is necessarily
an atheist. It is also interesting to note that the
host calls upon his servant, Pyrrhias, to con-
firm his account of the thirteen-hundred-foot-
high Hecate accompanied by " dogs taller than
Indian elephants " and of his detailed inspection, in the sudden chasm, of the denizens of
the Underworld. Pyrrhias had arrived on the
scene only as the chasm was closing, but he

readily confirms his master's story and adds that he had actually heard Cerberus barking. Thus the host's story is as well buttressed as that of any pseudo-psychist of today, citing concurrent testimony with a show of reasonableness.

Alexander the Fake-Prophet,[34] though exposing Lucian at his low-water mark of personal acrimony, is a useful milestone on the winding road of human credulity, essentially unchanged in eighteen hundred years. Granted our new scientific devices for staging, or for detecting ocular deceptions, any particular brand of imposture is merely a matter of detail.

But even some of the details, as narrated by Lucian, have a modern air. The new god,[35] neatly hatched before the very eyes of the gaping spectators from a goose-egg planted in the temple-foundation, grows in a few days into the huge tame snake which coiled affectionately around the prophet's body in a light as religiously dim as the beneficent darkness affected by contemporary mediums. The snake's own docile head was tucked under Alexander's armpit, and a counterfeit mouthpiece, worked by a skilful mechanism, protruded from the prophet's long beard.

[92]

The devices employed for discovering and answering the questions, submitted in sealed scrolls, were risky but, in spite of some awkward slips, yielded a large income. The *crux* of a growing, paying business in oracles was to deliver as few absurd ambiguities and as many plausible answers as possible. Although there was no " Who's Who in Paphlagonia " to furnish biographic clues, the clients were somewhat less sophisticated than our twentieth-century dupes, and shrewd guessing, aided, perhaps, by hypnotic suggestion and mind-reading, could accomplish much. The usual procedure, however, was to open the scrolls, keeping, by the help of a hot needle, the seal intact or, when necessary, skilfully forging new seals. The highest-priced oracular responses were " *autophones* " [36] delivered by a concealed assistant through a speaking tube debouching into the jaws of the counterfeit linen head of the snake.

One difference between then and now entitles us to some optimism. Lucian's injudicious unmasking of Alexander nearly cost him his life and necessitated an ignominious, though temporary, recantation. Now-a-days exposure proceeds in a scientific and progressive manner. Physicists and psychologists have responded to

the challenge made by a recrudescence of credulity and have laid bare many of the trickeries
of " levitation " and of messages from the dead,
made " evidential " by proleptic cramming of
biographic details. Even the pathetic frauds of
alleged " spirit " photographs have been, on
occasion, betrayed by the tell-tale lines of the
real newspaper original faithfully reappearing
on the lantern-slide. Finally, a scientist, himself a whilom dupe, has identified the ectoplasmic stuff that dreams were made of as the actual material output from a local manufactory.
Nor can we afford to be too contemptuous of
ancient superstition, for, while Alexander's
henchmen deceived high Imperial officials, our
own anachronistic credulity has not been altogether confined to the lowest order of intelligence. It has found lodgment in the brains
of well-known litterateurs or even, sporadically,
of a scientist deflected from sound reasoning by
personal bereavement.

3. Christianity

Lucian's references to Christianity have
been adequately discussed by commentators [37]
and there can be little difference of opinion as
to his attitude of kindly, though patronizing,

superiority towards one more set of contemporaries, misguided enough to believe in immortality. Apart from the two genuine works in which specific mention is made of the Christians there are a number of allusions, up and down his satires, which the supersensitiveness of the early church took as conscious slurs on the New or the Old Testament. Practically all of these are susceptible of another and easier interpretation.

Although Lucian was a Syrian by birth and evidently acquainted, by hearsay at least, with some of the facts of the crucifixion of Christ, the canon of the New Testament was not as yet established nor were its contents publicly circulated. Satire upon its tenets would not have made the wide and instant appeal to Lucian's audiences which was requisite for his purpose. His detailed description of the Islands of the Blest in the *True Story,* for example, would awaken welcome echoes of Pindar's second Olympic Ode or of the marvellous garden of Alcinoüs in the *Odyssey.* The detail of the vines which produce twelve crops annually and " yield fruit every month " seems now, to any reader of the New Testament, like an obvious loan from the *Apocalypse,* and it would be

risky to assert that this item could not have
been overheard by our Syrian at some Christian gathering. But, as a matter of literary
reminiscence, it would develop naturally, by
Lucian's favourite method of particularizing
details to give the effect of autopsy, from
Homer's own words:[38] " Of these the fruitage
never perishes nor even fails of winter or of
summer the whole year through; but aye and
ever does the Westwind blowing quicken these,
and ripen those; pear on pear grows ripe and
full, apple upon apple, clustered grape on grape
succeeding, fig on fig." He makes, for example,
in the interest of telling the *whole* truth, one
addition: " They said, however, that the pome-
granates, apple and other fruit trees produce
thirteen crops annually, for in one of their cal-
endar months, the month ' Minos,' they yield
two crops." [39] The " casting out of devils,"
also an apparent slur on the New Testament,
was more probably a generic reference to the
thriving practitioners of magic.

As to hits at Old Testament stories, the
chronological margin is elastic enough but the
supposed references are not convincing. Lucian, in the *True Story,* did not have to enlarge
the acreage of the interior of Jonah's " whale "

to make room for the truck-garden of Skin-
tharos within his big sea-monster; and, again,
the sudden chasm of air that interrupts his
boat's course comes from his own brilliant
fancy, not from the book of Exodus. The Bib-
lical crossing of the Red Sea would be, at best,
a very incomplete parallel.

Whatever degree of possibility, or probability, may be assigned to such covert reminiscences, the actual references to the Christians
make Lucian a favourable, because uninten-
tional, witness. In the *Alexander*, the charlatan
" prophet " includes the Christians with the
Epicureans in his most bitter anathemas:
" Away with the Christians! Away with the
Epicureans!" But it is precisely in the *Alexander* that Lucian most openly lauds Epicurus
and the Epicureans, and contrasts their uncompromising opposition to shams and superstitions with the perfect harmony existing between Alexander and the Stoic, Pythagorean
and Platonic schools! The Christians, therefore, were in the best company that he could
offer.

In the *Life's End of Peregrinus*, the Cynic
philosopher, craving notoriety and needing fi-
nancial support, is represented as having joined

the Christian sect after all other means of self-advertisement had grown stale and unremunerative. A certain real ability — for he was, after all, an accredited Cynic — raised him rapidly to prominence among the simpler folk of the Christian brotherhood. He expounded and, according to Lucian, even wrote some of their sacred books! He was called a " New Socrates " and his wants were well supplied. When cast into prison as too noisy a propagandist, he fairly lived in clover. These " non-professionals," who " hold all things in common," were easily duped by a professional charlatan like Peregrinus. " At short notice," says Lucian, " they contribute everything without reserve." " For," he continues, " these misguided persons have persuaded themselves that they are going to be altogether immortal and are going to live through time unending. In comparison with this the most of them despise death and voluntarily give themselves up to it. Then, too, their first lawgiver persuaded them that they are all brothers, one of the other, after they have once thrown over and denied the gods of Greece and have done reverence to that crucified sophist himself and live according to his laws."

Neither here nor elsewhere is Lucian making an attack on the Christians *per se*. Indeed, he poses almost as their partisan in his indignation against Peregrinus and his successful use of their simplicity. His patronizing contempt for their gullibility (as he saw it), led him to immortalize some of the most lovable and characteristic traits of the early brotherhood, and the church authorities of the sixteenth century seem short-sighted in placing on the *Index librorum prohibitorum* a tractate that might have been exploited as impartial testimony in their favour.

VII. OTHER DRAMATIC DIALOGUES: POLEMICS: NARRATIONS

MORE than twenty other writings of Lucian offer contributions necessary for an estimate both of his defects and of his versatile interest in the " passing show " — the human comedy. He was neither a master intelligence like Aristotle — expert in several of the many subjects to which he addressed himself — nor was he a mere polymath like Pliny the Elder or Aelian. In spite of his jaunty treatment of philosophy and exact science, Lucian at least takes cognizance of the chief components of contemporary life and with his mordant wit etches the portraiture of a great century. This is not mere caricature.

(a) DRAMATIC DIALOGUES

Under this rubric might be included the majority of the dialogues cited above to illustrate specific objectives of Lucian's satire. Some of the best dialogues, however, fall outside of the previous classification. To emphasize outstanding merit three titles are here treated separately.

The Cock

This is second to none of Lucian's dialogues in dramatic vigour. The flashes of wit and the sustained and entrancing humour of the situation are hardly equalled even in the *Icaromenippus*. The interjected sermonizing may be tedious, perhaps, to the mercurial modern, craving his " quick lunch," but so are the long, brilliant speeches of the *messenger* in Greek tragedy — and, for that matter, much of Shakespeare himself.

The general theme of the *Cock or the Dream* is contentment. Micyllus the cobbler, with whom we become intimate elsewhere, supports the rôle of righteous poverty. The account of his first and only dinner at a rich man's table contrasts the inequalities in human conditions. He is, in a dream, living over again the fleeting splendour of this banquet when he is awakened by the crowing of his officious cock who replies to his master's angry reproaches by a perfectly reasonable remark, made in excellent Greek. Indignation naturally gives place to amazement as the bird calmly explains his possession of human speech. He is Pythagoras, it seems, in addition to many other aliases. His soul, in fact, has lived through many transmigrations, brute and human, man and woman, with powers unimpaired. As Euphorbus, in the time of the Trojan War, he knew much more about Helen than did Homer who, at the time, was a mere Bactrian camel! After Pythagoras he was Aspasia, but admits that the rôle of Chanticleer is preferable to that of a mother-hen, so to say. Next he was the Cynic Crates, an expert pick-lock. This fact doubtless accounts for the special form of magic which he presently exhibits, albeit his inbred piety ascribes this power to Hermes, the Lord of Looting. The cock, as it transpires, can at will turn his long, curved, right-hand tail-feather into a master-key and this same night, before dawn, he takes the cobbler unseen through three rich men's houses. The cock, in various rebirths, had played many parts — rich man, poor man, king, horse, jackdaw *et al*. His experience of life is all-embracing. He tells the cobbler that, as a matter of fact, he has never seen anyone living more happily than Micyllus himself. " Than I, Cock? " the cobbler exclaims, " I wish you the same! Excuse me, please, but you forced out this curse." In the end, however, Micyllus is convinced. He learns the lesson of contentment.

When they start on their rounds the cobbler plucks out *both* the curving tail-feathers, explaining to the bereaved rooster that he wishes to make doubly sure of the key to the situation, adding that this precaution will also prevent the cock from being lop-sided. In the first house entered Simon, his *nouveau riche* neighbour, is seen, sleepless from fear of burglars, uncovering and counting and burying again his gold — a pale, worn miser. After a brief visit to a rich Shylock's house the magic feather next unlocks the door of Eucrates. Here the cobbler dined a few hours ago and all this gold-plate and other magnificence he had just inherited in his dream when awakened prematurely by the cock. As Micyllus enters the house he is once more dazzled by the splendour and exclaims: " All this was mine a little while ago!" Presently, however, he sees Eucrates, here betraying himself by his own passions, and here betrayed by his unfaithful wife. It is enough. The breaking dawn curtails the feather's magic and irradiates the beauty of the honest cobbler's daily toil.

Timon the Misanthrope

In this dialogue Lucian rehearses his familiar attacks on parasites, philosophers, rhetoricians, and the futility of the shopworn gods themselves. The *Timon* is accounted by some competent critics as Lucian's masterpiece, though he allows the caricature of the orator Demeas to become farcical, thus marring the artistic verisimilitude of the piece and, to this extent, putting it on a lower level than the *Charon,* or the *Cock*. But the dialogue marches to its goal — the creation [40] in literature of the typical Misanthropist. This involves, along with the dramatic, though incidental, punishment of the ungrateful parasites, the far greater punishment of Timon himself in becoming a full-fledged Egoist. To this egoism both poverty and riches contribute.

Lucian ignored Plutarch's data, if he knew them, and is not diverted from his main purpose by attributing any real virtue to Timon that could stand the strain of either riches or poverty. In the revamped Shakespearian play the centre of gravity is shifted to Timon's earlier days of prosperity and his good-natured prodigality is half confused with philanthropy, as reflected in the sympathy of the loyal and lovable Flavius. One of the " authors " of the *Timon of Athens,* indeed, outdoes Lucian by the cynical touch of subventions to the poisonous harlots, but he shuffles Timon off the stage, before he is fairly established as a practising misanthrope, and then deflects our attention to extraneous matter.

Lucian's neatest bit of satire, perhaps, is the egoism of Zeus, who rewards Timon simply and solely for his generous offerings, on Thanksgiving days, of fat bulls and goats. " Their savour," he naïvely remarks, " is still in my nostrils." The punishment of the ungrateful parasites must wait till he can have his thunderbolt repaired. Two of its tines were broken recently by striking the rock at the " Anaceum " temple instead of a sinner. For very bull-headedness Zeus never could hit the bull's-eye.

The personification of the blind god, Wealth, gives Lucian a grateful opportunity both for ethical observations and for picturesque geographical details, and his open and skilful use of the *Plutus* of Aristophanes only enhances his own dramatic creation.

The Dialogues of the Sea

In these fifteen aquarelles satirist and artist blend. Our ductile vision is refracted by the shining water and everything is credible within its magic depths. The artistic charm is permeated, but never marred, by a delicate satire, less obvious than the grim derision in the *Dialogues of the Dead*. While mocking at canonical mythology Lucian here reaches his end by no crass caricature but, ever and anon, Fancy astride a dolphin rises from the blue sea that holds the unnoticed satire in solution.

Several of these dialogues were pretty certainly suggested [41] by works of art extant in Lucian's time. Others would probably find their motive, or parallel, in paintings or sculpture now lost. Here, as elsewhere, Lucian illustrates the freemasonry of the brush, the chisel and the pen.

Within each tiny dialogue there is condensed a nucleus. Sometimes there are two centres of interest. Now, it is Polyphemus's brute strength succumbing to intellectual cunning and, inlaid upon it, the mimicry of Homer's ram; now, the cool bubbling fountain, worthy of Horace; now, the statuesque beauty of the

girl with her waterjar; now, the rescue of Andromeda, with the inimitable detail of the sea-
monster's bi-focal death — some of him slain
outright by the falchion of Perseus, and " as
much of him as had seen the Medusa " petri-
fying independently! Again, we have two pictures of Europa carried off by Zeus, incognito
as milk-white bull — a favourite model from
Ovid to Titian and Tennyson. Lucian's setting
is his own. The unlucky Southwind, assigned
that day to the Indian ocean, has missed this
lovely Mediterranean spectacle — the most
" magnificent sea-processional," Westwind tells
him, " that I have ever seen since I live and
have my blowing!"

The attention first centres on Europa, bullied
into an unwitting elopement. Then comes the
wedding-march. Only the more attractive sub-
marine life, such as tritons, dolphins and half-
naked Nereids, is allowed to show even a peri-
scope above the glassy surface. Poseidon, as
best man, convoys his swimming brother, and
Aphrodite, quite in her element, lolls back in
her sea-car, the fairest and most nonchalant
flower-girl that ever scattered roses from nearby Rhodes. As the handsome bull's front
hooves strike the beach he changes into the

divine bridegroom and the marines circum-
spectly submerge, setting the water a-boil.
" And I," says the envious Southwind, " was
looking at griffins, elephants, and black-a-
moors!"

In the Danaë seascape, finally, is a picture
that Simonides himself cannot blur from our
memory — the blue Aegean; the little ark; the
fair and smiling child; the fairer mother; the
brawny, gentle fishermen. Thetis, in a sub-
marine chat with Doris, tells how Danaë put up
no prayer for herself, when exposed on the sea
with Perseus, " but tried to beg off her baby
from death by shedding tears, as she holds it
out to its grandfather, and it was just the
prettiest little thing! And the baby, unconscious of ills, breaks into smiles at the sight of
the sea. ' Why my eyes are filled again with
tears, Doris, as I but remember them!' "

(b) POLEMICS

Alexander the Fake-Prophet is one of two
bitter polemics in which Lucian openly names
the person attacked. This has already been discussed in the chapter on the " Supernatural."
The piece, however, contains much additional
matter of interest. This, at least, should be

THE SNAKE-GOD GLYKON

From bronze statuette and cast of coin, struck under Lucius Verus, in the
BOSTON MUSEUM OF FINE ARTS.

See Note 35.

added. After due allowance is made for personal animosity the account does not seem to be a caricature and is partially confirmed by extant medals and a bronze-figure.[42] It may be used as furnishing data, essentially credible, for the diagnostician of human credulity.

The Life's-End of Peregrinus is also an attack upon a contemporary whose name is given and whose spectacular suicide is recorded by several unimpeachable authorities.[43] It is noteworthy not only for the allusions to the Christians, cited above, but also for the diagnosis of a man possessed with the demon of self-advertisement; for the psychology of the deceiving philosophers and their deceived contemporaries; for archaeological data — the picturesque references to the Games and to the terrain of Olympia should be read on the spot —; and, finally, the vivid narration, including the death-scene, the construction of the pyre, the sorrowing but self-possessed disciples, the pale philosopher, stripped to his shirt (" decidedly dirty " according to Cynic convention), weakening at the last moment but spurred on to the irrevocable act by the relentless admonition: " Go on with your programme!" This fling comes from one of the brotherhood who is already banking on the marketable value to the Cynic sect of the canonization of a self-immolated martyr. Lucian, indeed, anticipates the hatching of their chicken by letting an anapaestic vulture fly up in advance from the Cynic's ashes, chanting:

The Earth I have left, to Olympus I fare!

One thing only in this whole portrayal is open to question but that, unfortunately, is a matter of major importance. The self-immolation is amply attested by others but the character of Peregrinus is lauded by Aulus Gellius. Was he, at worst, only a fanatic or was he an imposter bitten by greed for glory? Is Lucian repeating unsupported gossip or even actual calumnies when he refers nonchalantly to various unsavoury episodes, including his murder of his father and his parasitical connection with the Christians? We cannot say, although it is an important factor in our estimate of Lucian himself. But the amiable assumption of Gellius, the myopic grammarian, is not demonstration. It does not prove either for his day or for our own that lofty sentiments must necessarily be sincere. Our golden idol may have feet of clay. Lucian, on the other hand, seldom identifies himself with Charity that "thinketh no evil."

Lucian, in fact, was not properly a biographer. The *Life of Demonax*, for example, if written by him, is dull. From Plutarch, whose honest shade had joined his mighty dead about the time of Lucian's birth, he may have drawn various hints but he made no nearer approach to his biographies than occasional juxtapositions like that of Alexander with Hannibal and Scipio in the *Dialogues of the Dead*. Nor need we count as biography the rhetorical " whitewashing " of the infamous Phalaris. The story, too, about Herodotus, retailed in the " curtainraiser " that bears his name, is an isolated, though interesting, item that reënforces Lucian's undisguised admiration for the incomparable charm of the incorrigible " Storyteller."

The Coach in Rhetoric

This diatribe is apparently directed against a real person. His actual name is suppressed but the reference to Castor and Pollux is almost sufficient [44] identification. Julius Pollux, a cheap but self-confident rhetorician, would seem, as appointee of the Emperor Commodus to the official Chair of Rhetoric in Athens, to

have aroused the contempt of the intelligentsia.
It is unnecessary to assume that Lucian himself was an unsuccessful rival for the place. If
half of the caricature were essentially representative it would justify his indignation as a sincere lover of good language and literature even
if the frank personalities were as untrue as they
are unnecessary.

The *Coach in Rhetoric* purports to be the
advice given gratis by a charlatan " professor "
to a neophyte seeking a short-cut to the same
showy success. Condensed from Lucian's bitter
gibing his advice, in fine, is to ignore the old-
fashioned, out-of-date disciplinary training.
None of that is needed or even desirable. The
easy road is also the shortest. Bold elocution,
brassy assertion, arrogant physical bearing are
the winning cards. You can begin at once. Not
even a psychological test is necessary, let alone
exact knowledge of anything. This has a familiar sound. If Lucian could have subordinated vituperation to his incisive wit and inescapable satire, and had made this attack in
his best manner, we might use it to draw an
easy and useful parallel by substituting for
" Rhetorician " our own denatured term " Edu-
cator."

The *Lexiphanes,*[45] or phrase-monger, is in a vein already opened up in the preceding piece. The would-be Atticist who injects into the matrix of vulgar Greek far-fetched Attic gems, which often turn out to be paste imitations, was typical of the imperfect imitators of Attic Greek who eagerly sought to excel in this contemporary, artificial Atticism.

Whether Pollux, as a charlatan "Commissioner of Education," or the whole breed of pretenders was the subject of this attack, Lucian, the expert Atticist, had a well-earned right to his contemptuous satire.

We cannot pursue further Lucian's philological polemics,[46] but any reader of Greek may derive pure fun in philology from the *Suit of Sigma against Tau.* This amusing little piece carries us out of the sorry milieu of human polemics into the miniature cock-pit of the letters of the alphabet. The Privy Council of the Vowels holds its sitting. At the end we are ready to crucify this accursed T on his own cross. If the piece is not, as has been suggested,[47] by Lucian himself we should like to read more by the same writer.

The Illiterate Bibliophile

This diatribe is directed against an unnamed but actual contemporary, a fellow Syrian, an ostentatious book-collector who is too ignorant to appraise the niceties of Attic style or even to read intelligently the contents of his costly collection. Like many a so-called " bibliophile " today, his love for books extends only to their external and marketable assets, such as: Copies by So and So; or their physical format, *e.g.*, a very beautiful scroll with purple vellum " jacket " and " golden knobs " on the end of the cylinder. The ugly personalities, in which Lucian sees fit to indulge, even if true, are beside the point. The rest of his incisive satire, changing certain details, is not out of date.

The collector's passion, however, is not confined to books which he never reads. He also collects relics. Among his exhibits, and procured for one thousand dollars plus, is the staff of the precious Cynic suicide, Peregrinus Proteus, thrown aside when he leaped into the fire. To show up all such futility Lucian rehearses how the tyrant Dionysius hoped to improve his literary style by procuring the very writing-tablets upon which Aeschylus had first

jotted down in Sicily some of his tragedies —
useless as the lyre of Orpheus without Orpheus,
or, in modern terms, as a *Stradivarius* without
the skilled musician!

How Should History be Written?

This informal letter begins with flaying contemporary would-be historians and gives illustrations of their brazen ignorance of facts,
their untruthfulness, their vanity, or parasitical
praise of patrons. Diogenes comes on the
scene, bowling his tenement-*jar* up and down
the market-place in Corinth, cynically mocking the ill-directed activities of his fellow-
citizens who were preparing to repel an inva-
sion. How *not* to write history was a congenial
theme for Lucian's destructive criticism. Addressing himself, in the second part, to the constructive side, and conscious of his unusual
rôle, Lucian says, deprecatingly: " I, too, roll
my jar!" His formulae are unstable under the
blow-torch of modern historical research. He
treats somewhat sketchily preliminary training
and also the sifting of facts and their sources,
but demands " political insight " and " faculty
of expression " along with unwavering independence of spirit and loyalty to Truth. He

would like to combine all the charm of Herodotus with the terse objectivity of Thucydides, whom he names specifically as the model.

Were it not so evident that the graces of style and diction are, for him, of such overmastering importance we could hardly demand of his age a higher conception of history. As it is, some modern non-professional readers may agree that historical characters are not " prisoners at the bar." To illustrate the Thucydidean belief that history must be inscribed on the bed-rock of Truth, he tells the effective story how on the veneered surface of the base of the Pharos light-house the architect attributed, by an inscription, its construction to the reigning Ptolemy, knowing well that the perishable exterior would, at some time safely remote, peel off and reveal to posterity his own name and fame.

(c) NARRATIONS

Though Lucian's skill in narration emerges in other types of writing it has free play in his *True Story*. This serves, indeed, as complement to the polemic just cited, but it is not so much a sequel as it is an antidote — a dose of hellebore against all boredom. He makes his own explanation of his purpose. After paying his respects to the purveyors of myths and histories, modern and ancient,[48] from the *Odyssey* on, he says: " Wishing to play my part in the world of letters and liars, and having no facts to recount — since nothing worth recording has ever happened to me — I will say in advance this one true thing, to wit, that I am going to tell you lies. So, then, I write about what I neither saw nor experienced nor heard of from others and, what's more, about things that never happen at all nor could happen."

With this premised, we take ship with Lucian and pass through " The Straits " into the uncharted West. Atlas, vainly trying to hold asunder the divinely wedded Earth and Heaven, drops behind the horizon and, after some preliminary adventures, our seaplane is whirled aloft into the heavenly hemisphere. All earthly cares are jettisoned. Later, indeed, we have brief glimpses of home affairs reflected in the magic mirror of the Moon, or seen by the light of our own family lamp, encountered while it is taking a day off in Lamp-heaven, but none of these things ruffle our high celestial content.

Lucian's conceits rarely degenerate into burlesque. Through the whole narrative he holds us captive by his air of verisimilitude. His magical imagination does not travel on the stilts of magic — that hard-worked *deus ex machina* of tales like *Kalevala* — for Magic itself is only one more quarry [49] for his falcon wit. Even in his frequent recourse to exaggeration his surprises vary. The monstrous fish, for example, gulps down unharmed Lucian's ship, crew and all, down through his roomy throat, past another · vessel, lying there a derelict. Within, there are forests and fields and hostile tribes. There is a lake and a vegetable garden cultivated by a Crusoe and his son, long since interned. The escape attempted by tunnelling the right-hand wall of the huge crypt makes a relatively insignificant dent and is abandoned after excavating for five-eighths of a mile! The ship is finally hauled up and lowered into the sea by using as davits the monster's huge teeth. The vessel slips through the interstices as easily as might a strand of dentist's floss. Again, in the Island of Dreams, he finds that Homer was wholly inadequate in limiting the " Doorways for Dreams " to two only — the " horn " and the " ivory." As a matter of fact there were four! Or Rhadamanthus embarks fifty heroes to pursue Helen, who is again eloping, in a long-boat hewn from a single log of asphodel — a monoxyl! The slender asphodel, it seems, knows no girth-control under the never-ending sunshine in the Island of the Blessed.

Or his method may be to invert reality. The questing ship, for example, comes suddenly to a crevasse, yawning in its path, and is checked just in time before it plunges over the edge into the chasm of air.[50] This chasm, however, is presently crossed on a Natural Bridge of water, sighted nearby, which unites precariously, on the surface, the severed cliffs of water.

Lucian prolongs our appetite by the recurrent intellectual spice of delicate parodies. Just at the end he draws aside his rainbow veil to show us the ass's shins of reality and bows us, breathless, back again into " our own continent that lies opposite."

It would be easy to make other detached excerpts but only by reading the whole can we fully appreciate how, with gathered momentum, the *True Story* has stimulated the long line of imitators who also have smuggled through the " ivory gate " their lesser share of celestial loot.

Familiarized with the flavour of Lucian's narration in the *True Story*, the *Lie-Fancier*, the *Icaromenippus,* the *Toxaris* and other writings, it is tempting to accept as genuine the *Syrian Goddess* and the *Ass.* The *Syrian Goddess,*[51] flaunting her oriental nakedness through the diaphanous Ionic dress, has touches of humour that suggest a deliberate satire on the naïveté of Herodotus and on the current fad for Ionicizing, notwithstanding some linguistic flaws foreign to Lucian's style. *Lucius or the Ass* [52] is apparently an epitome of a lost original. Lapses into the vulgar dialect betray a different hand (or, perhaps, an artistic whim), but long stretches of narration in this famous and outrageous tale suggest that Lucian is lurking in person within the ass, availing himself with gusto of this excellent chance to satirize the current belief in magic.

The identical matter of certain passages in this and in Apuleius's *Golden Ass* presupposes an archetype.[53] Whether this was written by Apuleius or, as it has been argued, by Lucian himself, the brilliant Syrian was no mere plagiarist and whatever part he may have had in telling, or retelling, the tale, the purpose underlying his facile narration was the mockery of credulity. He was a lion in an ass's skin!

VIII. LUCIAN'S CREDITORS AND DEBTORS

1. SOURCES

IN THE case of authorship antedating the honest confessional of the footnote or the scholar's page, sicklied o'er with conscientious references, the identification of indebtedness, varying from conjecture to certainty, is a fascinating and, at times, an illuminating pursuit.

Fully to tabulate Lucian's obligations to predecessors and, perhaps, to contemporaries is not now practicable. He is openly proud of his debt to classic Greek writers but is normally reticent about obligations to Roman predecessors, or to contemporaries, whether Greek or Roman. His writings abound in parodies, full quotation, and interwoven scraps of citation. In all this the intended effect would depend largely upon the instant recognition by his audience of the original. For example, the second *Dialogue of the Sea*, except for those familiar with the *Odyssey*, would lack meaning when, with Lucianic additions, the Cyclops rehearses to his father, the naïve Poseidon, the story of Odysseus and the ram. This would, in turn, recall the inimitable parody in the *Wasps* of Aristophanes, where the jury-maniac, Philocleon, essays escape under the shaggy belly of the family donkey.

The revamping of plot or of whole characters from the Attic drama would be more than an extension of this form of intentional reminiscence. The title of Lucian's *Timon* was not improbably suggested by the *Timon* of Antiphanes, not now extant. This, however, in itself proves nothing. Just as " Electra " changed her robes under the hands of her three distinguished *couturières* of the fifth century, so we find in the Comic Fragments more than 250 identical titles reappearing respectively in the writings of from two to eight different authors. As a matter of fact, it is to the *Plutus* of Aristophanes that we turn to enjoy, in Lucian's *Timon,* his adroit use of a predecessor. The result was not a mere *contaminatio.* We may assume the same with the *Charon,* or the *Cock.* Their effect upon the mind renders incredible the suggestion that they are not fresh-minted. If in his *Charon,* for example, Lucian had some

" original " in mind we do not need to know it, either for understanding or for enjoyment. It would, however, make a difference in our estimate if it could be shown that our author slavishly or clandestinely imitated, in form or in substance, works now no longer extant. Should we give to Menippus, for example, the real credit for the creation of the Satiric Dialogue? Are the *Necyomanteia,* the *Dialogues of the Dead,* the *Cronos Letters,* the orgiastic satire in the *Symposium,* and elements in the *Hermotimus,* etc., plagiarisms? We cannot be dogmatic in each case but it is at least obvious that the frequent references to Menippus would have sufficiently recalled writings that were still accessible. Lucian was content with his own originality and submits his book-keeping for inspection in open court. Modern critics most entitled [54] to an opinion rank Lucian among the great, though not the greatest, creative writers of antiquity.

In general, it seems safe to conclude that Lucian regarded the writings of predecessors and contemporaries as an open quarry from which he first built up his own style and then picked out material to imbed, with an artist's skill, in the parti-coloured mosaic of his satire.

Such material, drawn here and there from the *Wonders of the Island Thule* of Antonius Diogenes [55] or from Theopompus before him, or from the pious Plutarch, or from the elusive sources of the *Arabian Nights* or other oriental tales, may have been freely transferred to his *True Story* without implying plagiarism any more than did his parodies on the *Odyssey*. Even the *Ass* by " Lucius of Patrae," if we discover the Lucianic stigmata beneath its shaggy hair, would justify itself, contrasted with the " golden " credulity of Apuleius, as a pungent satire on the current belief in magic.

Whether Lucian is to be accredited with the creation or only the development of the Satiric Dialogue is a different matter. This, in a sense, calls in question his originality. Perhaps the first suggestion for his brilliant *Sale of Sample Lives* came from a dialogue of Menippus, entitled the *Sale of Diogenes*. Croiset, however, justly remarks:[56] " si Lucien l'a imité, ce n'a été qu'en se reservant le droit de la transformer " — the quality of this transformation is, in the last analysis, the essential thing.

Latin Sources

The identification in Lucian's writings of direct reminiscences from Latin writers is precarious when so much of the content of literature and tradition had passed into community ownership but, apart from the argument *ex silentio,* which would be as misleading here as elsewhere, there is no good reason to ignore Lucian's own words and to assume that he could not use freely such Latin writings as were physically available.

Certain passages reflect, some certainly, some with more or less probability, the thought or actual words of Lucretius, Virgil, Horace, Tacitus, Juvenal, Ovid and Pliny. A number of such reminiscences or parallels have been pointed out by various[57] scholars. By way of supplement it may be remarked here that the details, even verbal, in Lucian's description of Phaëthon (number twenty-five of the *Dialogues of the Gods*), read like a racy synopsis of Ovid's words. The contacts with Ovid's poetry are numerous and Lucian, who compares himself to an Attic bee questing for honey, would have noted Ovid's exquisite verses[58] fragrant with memories of Mt. Hymettus. In the *Charon* the falling tile which prevents the dinner-guest from keeping his engagement, has an obvious parallel in Juvenal's third satire. This particular type of accidental death was, indeed, so common that we cannot claim from this incident alone an actual reminiscence, but the community of feeling throughout the corresponding scene in Juvenal reënforces the antecedent probability that Lucian was familiar with the Roman satirist.

Suggestions from Works of Art

Among Lucian's creditors we must also include sculptors, painters and architects. His obligations, however, in the realms of art, other than his own, would require a separate treatise.[59] When he discusses, either incidentally or of set purpose, actual works of art, his comments are so incisive that he has been characterized as " undoubtedly the most trustworthy art-critic of antiquity." [60] This discriminating apperception of truth and beauty, in form and design, was an integral part of his mental equipment. We feel this discrimination in his visualization of a certain portrait statue, otherwise unknown,—" a pot-bellied man, hair receding on the forehead, half-naked, some

hairs of his beard wind-tossed, outstanding
veins, a man to the very life " — no less than
in his vivid sketches of world-famous statues
like Myron's *Discobolus,* the *Cnidian Aphrodite,* the *Diadumenus,* or the *Tyrant-slayers.*
His inspiration, too, from pictorial art was important. He welcomes the opportunity, for example, to give a " word-picture " of the *Centaur Family* by Zeuxis (though from a copy of
the original) which is itself important in the
history of painting. Or again, we feel the impression made on his mind by the painter's art
in his catalogue of the paintings which adorned
the lecture auditorium of whose architectural
splendour, incidentally, he gives us a wordy
picture.

But quite apart from this incidental legacy
of art through description, more important for
our appreciation of Lucian are his elusive transfers, not always capable of identification, from
the medium of plastic and graphic art into such
word-pictures as the vignettes in the *Dialogues
of the Gods* and the *Dialogues of the Sea.* Obviously, in some instances, a telescoping of
sources — from both art and literature — may
be assumed. For the Europa [61] story, for example, there was abundant material in art, and

in literature in the accounts given by Moschus and twice by Ovid. In the *Rescue of Andromeda* Ovid represents Perseus as slaying the monster with his falchion only, while Lucian brings in also the Medusa head and follows the monuments of art (except the vases), as, for example, in the painting described by him in *The Hall* (22). This, of course, gives Lucian his chance for his characteristic persiflage.[62] Lucian's delight in placing the gods in a comic situation led him more than once into repetition. The sight of a statuette, as Blümner suggests, where a woman with upraised hand is threatening her victim with chastisement from her sandal, gave him, perhaps, the cue for the punishment of the naughty Eros by his mother (*Dialogues of the Gods*, 11. 1) and also for the lubberly Heracles brought under the sandal of Omphale (*Dial.*, 13. 2 and *How to Write History*, 10). Passing over other similar instances, we note in the *Charon* another suggestion from the field of art — if art it may be called. The ferryman is explaining why his ship's galley is so well-stocked with Homeric *hors d'oeuvres*. The poet, it seems, had grown suddenly sea-sick on the voyage and had left unclaimed in Charon's boat an ample chrestomathy, " including Scylla, Charybdis, and Cyclops." Lucian may have seen a picture made by Galato in the age of the Ptolemies representing the citations issuing from Homer's mouth while the lesser breed of poets were gathering up these " wingèd words " — these undigested " slices " from the Homeric menu!

Lucian, as coinheritor of Greek art, moved about continuously in a world of beauty, perhaps only " half-realized " even by our patient and pious reconstruction. He could see, day after day, the still virgin Parthenon and within it the gold-ivory Athena with Victory [63] on her extended hand. He could see in the Acropolis Picture Gallery and in the Cnidian Club at Delphi paintings of Polygnotus whose populous portrayal of the Underworld was catholic enough to include, for his benefit, Charon and the boat, as well as the ghostly *dramatis personae* from the *Odyssey*. And, across the Aegean, he could see the Cnidian Aphrodite herself — no mere reproduction where the copyist's defacing fingers have blurred the perfect work of Praxiteles.

As satirist Lucian seized his opportunities at will but the artist within him could respond just as seriously to the impacts of beauty from sculpture and painting as to the suggestions garnered from his own field of art — from prose and poetry.

2. LUCIAN'S LEGATEES

i. IN ART

IN THE field of art Lucian transmitted or originated suggestions for some of the greatest artists of Europe. Wherever these suggestions can be identified as themselves transmuted by Lucian from monuments of sculpture or, more frequently, from pictorial art, our interest is enhanced by the very continuity of motif.

It is not surprising that the fresh impulse given by the Revival of Greek, and the re-covery of Lucian among other writers, should have stimulated the imagination of Renaissance artists more effectively than did the abundant suggestions already at hand, for example, in the duller pages of the elder Pliny. Leone Battista Alberti (1404–1472), musician, painter, sculptor, architect, poet and prose-writer, was an enthusiastic intermediary. By a special tract on Lucian's description, in his *De Calumnia*, of the painting ascribed to Apelles he commended Lucian to the attention of artists as convincingly as Quintilian, in his day, had commended Menander to young Roman orators. Botticelli reconstructed Lucian's description in his immortal painting and was followed by Raphael, Mantegna and others.[64] Albrecht Dürer included the " Calumny of Apelles " among the designs furnished for the mural decorations in Nuremberg. Froben, in answer to the detractors of Erasmus, inserted in a second edition of the New Testament, as one of the illustrations, this still vigorous *Calumnia*. Rembrandt, or a pupil, still later reproduced Mantegna's motif. Botticelli also transferred, somewhat altered, to his canvas Lucian's description of the *Centaur Family* — a precursor of the landscape. In the Palazzo Borghese a pupil filled out Raphael's sketch (still extant) of Lucian's *Marriage of Alexander and Roxana,* which also formed the nucleus of Sodoma's splendid fresco in the Chigi house in Rome and was later to reappear from the fecund brush of Rubens.

The imaginative picture of " eloquence " in Lucian's *Gallic Heracles* emerges in sketches by Raphael, Dürer, and Holbein. Holbein also reproduced vividly Lucian's cashiered family-tutor and passed on the needed, long unheeded, warning to all literati who hang on patrons' favours.

In the *Nigrinus* of Lucian occurs the suggestion for the red-crayon drawing, by Michelangelo, of the archer shooting the " wingèd word " at his victim. From this drawing, found at Windsor Castle, a scholar of Raphael later made a fresco.

In Dürer's sketchbook in Vienna is preserved his " Europa " taken from the fifteenth *Dialogue of the Sea*. Titian's coarse lady, lolling on the bull, has only the subject in common with the delicate beauty of Lucian's description, happily retouched in perfect lines by Tennyson in his *Palace of Art*.

The *Dialogues of the Dead*, more than any other work by Lucian have furnished suggestions to pictorial artists. Death's toll is even more universal than the levy exacted by Eros. Hans Holbein's name is conventionally identified with the " Dance of Death." [65] Some representations of it have been incorrectly attributed to him.[66] He has even been falsely accredited with the invention of the motif itself. This subject was a favourite decoration for bridges as, for example, the arresting gable-paintings in the covered Pont des Moulins at

Lucerne; for churches and churchyards: for example, the Dominican convent at Bâle, Saint Mary's Church at Lübeck,[67] the "Triumph of Death" in the Campo Santo at Pisa; for houses, as the one at Bâle said to have been decorated by Holbein, or the frescoes said to have been painted by him for Henry VIII in the palace of Whitehall and burnt in 1697; or as decorations on ladies' fans — a beneficent *cave feminam!* The irony of Lucian's dialogues was also woven into the "Hans Holbein Alphabet," and it was Holbein who sketched the grim reminders on the margin of Erasmus's *Encomium Moriae* and who used them to illustrate Sir Thomas More's *Utopia.*

Observing all due precaution against making arbitrary identifications one might go on to gather other examples. Even a casual review of museum catalogues suggests, here and there, Lucian's influence, direct or indirect, upon pictorial art.

ii. IN LITERATURE

Reminiscence: Imitation: Parallels

Lucian's influence upon subsequent literature, in the sum total, has been very great,

[133]

greater, of course, at some periods than at others.[68]

Probably he influenced his younger contemporaries. What relation may have existed between him and Apuleius has not been determined past peradventure. It seems clear, however, that the vigour of both of them in story-telling, whatever their indebtedness to the *Odyssey* and to Herodotus or to Ovid himself, launched anew [69] the Story, as such, on its long voyage through the Middle Ages down to the modern novel.

The dates and data at our disposal are not always precise. Alciphron, for example, is variously treated as a younger contemporary or as a slightly later writer. The *Letter to Lucian,* included among his works, would seem, to the present writer, to indicate that the latter [70] assumption, rather than the former, were correct. In addition to their common debt to the New Comedy Alciphron betrays, on occasion, his indebtedness to Lucian.

Philostratus, writing in the third century, did not pay Lucian the doubtful compliment of including him in his " Lives of the Sophists," probably because he observed " the sophistic convention of silence as to the one who so ex-

celled and satirized them all." [71] Lucian, however, is conspicuous by the omission. He made
a fortunate and timely escape from this narrow
profession, but he is, none the less, inevitably
drawn by modern critics into comparison with
the Sophists.

Gregory of Nazianzes and John Chrysostom,
still reflecting a genuine Hellenism in the fourth
century, were able and willing to appreciate
Lucian in spite of his paganism.

The Emperor Julian found in Lucian because of his paganism a welcome ally in the
losing battle for a decadent Hellenism. And
Libanius, who had taught Chrysostom eloquence, and who was the much older contemporary and guide of Julian, in his voluminous
outpouring of wearisome rhetoric, could include
meaningless critiques upon Aristophanes and
Lucian while he makes use of the latter to give
flavour to his own insipid declamation. He is,
for example, borrowing from Lucian's brilliant
and scathing diagnosis of the *Hireling Professors* when, in his epideictic oration [72] on
the varied forms of human slavery, he dilates
upon the bondage of the " house-professor."
To satisfy father, mother, grandpa and grand-
ma the " professor," he says, must demonstrate

that their young hopeful is on a par with the sons of gods! Nor may he venture to ignore anyone in the whole *entourage* — not the door-tender, not the " male chaperone," not the servants who carry the boy's books, not even — note the present-day touch! — the athlete! A picture sordid enough, certainly, even for the twentieth century, and unenlivened by Lucian's caustic comments. It does, however, indicate the wholesome contempt to which the sophistic professor of mere rhetoric was again subjected in the fourth century, as contrasted with his unparalleled power and popularity in the time of Philostratus.[73] Thus the keen satire of Lucian, the " Apostate " from sophistic rhetoric, was already in process of vindication. Fast colours do not fade!

At the end of the third century and the beginning of this fourth century two other well-known writers, pro-Christian and pro-pagan respectively, testify that Lucian was present, at least, in the consciousness of both factions. Lactantius, the very respectable " Christian Cicero," speaks [74] of Lucian as one who spared neither gods nor men, while the inferior but useful Eunapius selects [75] for approval, because of its serious purpose, the dull *Demonax,* of doubtful authenticity though ascribed to Lucian the "expert in mockery."

As we penetrate deeper into the labyrinth of Byzantine literature we find Lucian secure in his place among Greek classics, either included directly by name or by the still more flattering praise of imitation. The large number of only partly edited "imitators" in the Paris and Vatican libraries, respectively,[76] might contribute further data, and the late and spurious *Philopatris,* foisted upon the Lucianic canon by an unknown tenth-century author, continued for centuries to involve Lucian in wholly unnecessary abuse from uncritical Christians.

Photius, in the ninth century, in addition to detailed comment, already mentioned, includes Lucian as an especial favourite in his list of prose authors. Luitprand, the "most original hellenist"[77] of the tenth century, quotes, *inter alia,* from Lucian's *Dream.*

Suidas, whose combined lexicon and encyclopaedia is referred to "the third quarter of the eleventh century,"[78] gives a genial and doubtless quite orthodox opinion as to Lucian's contemporary whereabouts. Lucian in his *Life's End of Peregrinus* had spoken in a patronizing, but by no means entirely uncomplimentary

manner of the Christians, referring, incidentally, to " that crucified sophist " of theirs. This
draws from the pious lexicographer specific details as to Lucian's death and subsequent career, closing with the words: " And in the time
to come he shall be joint heir with Satan of the
fire everlasting!" Of this much, at least, we
may be sure: the *Peregrinus* had not yet, as
was the case later, been cut out of the Lucian
manuscript accessible to Suidas.

Tzetzes in the twelfth century, in his huge
poem, nearly thirteen " chiliads " in length,
gives Lucian, of course, his due place among
some four hundred authors cited, from Homer
down to Byzantine times.[79]

The *Experiences of Timarion* in his visit to
the Underworld is also referred to the twelfth
century by Krumbacher and described as " one
of the numberless Byzantine imitations of Lucian " for, although the theme itself goes back
to the *Odyssey,* it is a direct revival in dialogue
form of Lucian's *Menippus* or *Necromancy.*
Incidentally the great ghost of Psellus, " the
Photius of the Eleventh century," is satirized
under a thin disguise.[80] This motif continued
to be a favourite. It reappears, for example, in
Mazaris's *Trip to Hades,*[81] about 1416 A.D.,

which is a combination of dialogue and letter-form and one of the more wooden imitations of Lucian.

Theodorus Prodromus [82] (1118–1180) stands at the very threshold of Modern Greek literature and wrote, indeed, both in the vulgar and in the Byzantine Greek. He was an inveterate polygraph in poetry and prose, ranging from rhetoric and theology, grammar and philosophy and astrology to the poetic romance and satire. His interest for us lies in the fact that he was apparently at his best when following Lucian, as in his loans from the *Tragical Zeus* and in his better-known satirical dialogue *The Sale of Philosophers and Statesmen,* which is an elaborate imitation of Lucian's brilliant *Sale of Soul Samples*. In this he sells off, amongst other parcels, Homer, Hippocrates, Aristophanes, Euripides and Demosthenes.[83]

Johannes Katrarius, sometimes referred to the tenth century but more probably of the twelfth or thirteenth,[84] may be allowed to close this summary selection from Byzantine writers.

The Latin conquest of Constantinople in 1204 A.D., made possible direct access to Greek learning without the intervention of the Arabic, while the infiltration into the West of a knowledge of the Greek language prepared the way for a Revival of Greek Learning, happily anticipating the actual occupation by the Turk, in the fifteenth century, of the moribund Byzantine Empire.

Lucian made his début in Italy toward the end of this period. Greater names received first attention but also, by the perversity of circumstance, authors inferior to him gained an earlier hearing. No other characteristic of these intellectual Crusaders is more pathetic than their lack of perspective in the reverence for any and every MS. recovered — any goose, Roman or Greek, became forthwith a swan! Petrarch, indeed, treasured a *Homer* and a *Plato* that he could not read and his *Letters to Dead Authors* do not reëcho Lucian's *Dialogues of the Dead*. Boccaccio, who could boast of being the first Italian to " resume " the reading of Homer, contented himself with Latin authors, like Ovid and Apuleius, when, if Lucian had been easily accessible, he might have found stimulus in him also.

To Aurispa of Sicily, who in 1423 brought some 238 Greek MSS. to Venice,[85] may be ascribed the introduction of Lucian into Italy. He was, however, less remarkable as a scholar than as a collector of MSS. and thought it a matter of plain patriotic duty, in translating Lucian's twelfth *Dialogue of the Dead,* to alter the original by assigning the first place to the Roman Scipio instead of to Alexander the Great! [86]

In this group of collectors, who were also translators of Lucian, may be mentioned: Filelfo, long resident in Constantinople, who, by way of perfecting his Greek, married the grand-niece of Chrysoloras, the first and greatest of the "visiting professors" of Greek; also the famous Poggio himself; and, with especial honour, Guarino da Verona, who not only imported in 1408 more than fifty MSS. but was also a sound and inspiring scholar. Among other works he translated at least three of Lucian's writings. Very early in the fifteenth century translations and citations in lectures from Greek authors took a wide range, as with Bruni and Marsuppini. For Lucian, in particular, several writers may be emphasized. Alberti, as above mentioned, stimulated by the association with graphic art, started, by his tractate on the *De Calumnia* of Lucian, this rather mediocre piece on its long and efficient career.

Matteo Maria Boiardo, towards the end of the fifteenth century, however, selected one of Lucian's most famous dialogues, *The Timon*, from which he developed a full-fledged comedy in verse, *Il Timone*,[87] with its lame and impotent dénouement. This, in turn, may have been indirectly laid under contribution in constructing the patch-work play, *Timon of Athens*, attached to Shakespeare's name, which, in spite of futile accretions, manages to preserve some of the original Lucianic colour. Be that as it may, Lucian transmitted from antiquity and standardized for the modern world a clear-cut type of the misanthrope.[88]

Pontano, also, who died in 1503, in his poetic satire, *Charon*, had Lucian's like-named dialogue [89] as forerunner.

Ariosto, the successor of Boiardo in more senses than one, is deeply in debt to Lucian. Of him and of two of his slightly younger contemporaries it has been remarked: [90] " The peregrinations of Ariosto and Folengo and Rabelais, the adventures of their heroes, the strange countries they visit, owe much more to Lucian . . . than to the quest of the New World, and the discovery of its wonders." By this time, in fact, Lucian had become very popular and Folengo's burlesque romance, *Baldus,* makes particularly clear the influence of the *True Story.*

When we pass from Italy to the north and west of Europe, in the latter part of the fifteenth and the beginning of the sixteenth centuries, it is embarrassing to attempt to catalogue and still more to classify rigidly the more significant names of Lucian's debtors. He stimulated, indeed, imaginative humour now with, now without, an ulterior motive of didactic satire. But, for the most part, the wanton joys of the pagan Revival in Italy are obscured in the cold transalpine mists of controversy. The satire of Lucian, the potential foe to all theologies, was a weapon available to opposing warriors in the joyless jousts of the Reformation.

The *editio princeps* of Lucian, printed in Florence, 1494–96, by Constantine Lascaris, made his writings the common property of scholars. Translation, citation, and imitation in Latin or even in the vernaculars, widened indefinitely his sphere of influence.

Desiderius Erasmus (1467–1536), whose reduplicated Graeco-Roman name could ignore all geographic barriers, is the best liaison be-

tween the members of the brilliant groups of
his immediate or younger contemporaries —
Dutch, English, French, German or Italian —
who perpetuated Lucian's influence. His lucid
Latin is not a borrowed tool. It is intellectually and stylistically his own. Incidentally,
he models on the *Lexiphanes* of Lucian his
dialogue, *Ciceronianus*,[91] in which he derides
the folly of a slavish imitation of a single
author. This sterling Latinity of his, good at
its face value for the " Latin Union " of the
European intelligentsia, was the medium
through which Lucian's best satire first " swims
into the ken " of many eager contemporaries.
Keen in distinguishing between the ephemeral
and the universal, Erasmus applied Lucian's
satire to current ethics and ecclesiastical practices. In addition to other minor pieces he
translated many of Lucian's vital writings,
including the *Cock*, the *Icaromenippus*,
Timon,[92] *Alexander the False Prophet*, the
Banquet, the *Hireling Professors* and the
Saturnalia, often sending them as gifts to
friendly patrons, before they were published,
along with others translated by his running
mate, Sir Thomas More. With generous enthusiasm he writes to another friend, Am-

monius, the Latin secretary of Henry VIII:
" I am delighted that you are Lucianizing." [93]
Loyal to his own religious beliefs, Erasmus
did not hesitate to use Lucian to scourge ecclesiastical shams, although charged, on the
one hand, with heresy and atheism by venal
and sensual clerics, or branded as a " second
Lucian " [94] by the dogmatic Luther. But Chris-
tendom would listen neither to " Right Reason " nor to satire. The antichristian spirit of
hate and persecution common to both parties,
precipitated the long orgy of blood and fire,
and in all the subsequent stagings of this
tragedy of religion Lucian's mocking laughter reëchoes, again and again, as the blood-
stained actors make their respective exits
down " Charon's Stairs " to take up their new
rôles, on the transstygian shore, as *dramatis
personae* in unpublished *Dialogues of the
Dead*.

Lucian's influence upon Erasmus is even
more important in writings other than his
direct translations. The *Praise of Folly,* which
electrified both the fools and the savants of
Europe, is charged with the Lucianic current.
In his priceless *Colloquia* Erasmus, like Lucian,
paints contemporary life in vivid colours but

is free from Lucian's taint of bitter pessi-mism.[95] He seasons his observations, however, as he says elsewhere,[96] with both *sal nigrum* and *sal candidum* from his Lucianic salt-cellar.

Lucianic reminiscences in the *Colloquia* may be culled almost at random. *The Exorcism* or *The Apparition*,[97] for example, is a good pen-dant to Lucian's *Lie-Fancier*, though the witty treatment is Erasmus's own; *The Female Parliament*,[98] though patterned after Aristoph-anes, contains almost more of Lucian; *The Charon*,[99] along with the Lucianic matter, in-cludes suggestions of Aristophanes. But Eras-mus is not hampered by his models. Charon's boat, old and rotten by this time, has just foundered. Charon himself has made land, dripping from his immersion; his late pas-sengers, the ghosts, are still swimming with the *Frogs!* A new transport must be built, too staunch to be sunk by papal bulls or other ecclesiastical fauna smuggled on board. As to motive power the ghosts, whether commoners, monarchs or cardinals, reduced as they are to the least common denominator of democ-racy, will have to do the rowing. The chief hitch is that there is no wood for shipbuilding, as the Elysian forests have been consumed in the burning of heretics!

Among the many comments in the *Epistles*, Erasmus's reference to the *Hireling Professors* emphasizes a condition as acute in his day as in Lucian's.[100] The impecunious litterateur was more or less dependent on powerful patrons. Erasmus himself was no complete exception to the rule, but it is to his everlasting credit that he rejected the temptation to exchange his poverty and independence for a life of luxury and power. He refused to become a " red-hatted lackey of the Holy See." [101] Lucian's scathing and witty sermon on the hireling doubtless helped him to save alive his own soul. He could honestly continue to preach from Lucian's texts. Again and again through the centuries literary semi-parasites ruefully, and almost involuntarily, confess the truth of Lucian's picture.

Sir Thomas More's Latin translations from Lucian, inspired by Erasmus and inserted in his volume, included the *Cynic*, the *Menippus* or *Necromancy* and the *Lie-Fancier* (*Philopseudes*). More's own comments [102] are illuminating. Despite his unshakable devotion to the authority of the Church, for which he was to suffer martyrdom, he could, at this period, welcome the keen satire of Lucian as a prophylactic. Even St. Chrysostom, he says in reply to heckling ecclesiastics, included the *Cynic,* in part, in one of his homilies as a protest against luxury and self-indulgence, while St. Augustine had been misled by some imposter to accept as a Christian miracle what Lucian had ridiculed, under a different name, many years before him in the *Philopseudes.*

More's *Utopia,* which also belongs to Latin, not to English, literature, reflects, quite apart from Plato and St. Augustine, the humour and imagination of Lucian's *True Story.* It was translated into foreign vernaculars before it was done into English.[103]

Of this transition to the vernacular, with its modicum of incidental " Lucianizing," we are also inevitably reminded by the " delectable dog-Latin " [104] of the anonymous *Epistolae Obscurorum Virorum* pitted, on occasion, against the full-dress Latin of Erasmus and Reuchlin. Two hundred years later, *per contra,* Voltaire, in *Les trois empereurs en Sorbonne,* resurrects Marcus Aurelius and others to shudder at the Latin of the theologians! In these dialogues, at any rate, is reflected Lucian's mastery of the special form of mockery, where would-be defendants, whether gods or men, plead guilty by explaining.

The dramatic dialogue *Eckius Dedolatus*,[105] published anonymously about 1530, is a not wholly negligible addition to this literary form descended from Plato, via Lucian, to the *Colloquia* of Erasmus. Its content, also, now reminiscent of Lucian, now anticipating the coarser humour of Rabelais, is germane to our discussion.

The great German [106] humanists knew and used Lucian, whose satire was as flexible as Holy Writ itself for purposes of controversial citation. Johann Reuchlin, erudite linguist and crusader against the Obscurantists, found time to do some translating from the *Dialogues of the Dead*.[107] The satiric dialogue, with actual Lucianic content, became the most effective weapon for Ulrich von Hutten.[108] He wrote first in Latin but enlarged his audience by a later transfer to the vernacular, such as it then was. He made use of Lucian's *Cataplus* (or " Crossing the Bar "); later, in his *Phalarismus,* he tipped with venom from Lucian's *Tyrant* the darts aimed at Duke Ulrich von Wittenberg; he modelled on Lucian's *Hireling*

Professors a dialogue against servility to patrons; drew on the *Dialogues of the Dead* and notably on the *Charon;* and left for post-humous publication his *Arminius,* modelled on the favourite twelfth *Dialogue of the Dead.* Still more to the point, he is generally accredited with being one of the three joint authors of the *Dialogi Virorum Obscurorum.*

Philip Melanchthon (1497–1560), the brilliant young Greek scholar, an admirer and friend of Erasmus in his youth but later a partisan of Luther, translated from the Greek Lucian's *De Calumnia* for his controversy at Wittenberg, just as, conversely, he had Graecized his own German name, Schwarzerd.

Among the numerous recruits to Lucianic interpretation Jacob Molsheym of Strasburg deserves especial mention for two reasons. He was a versatile contributor to both Greek and Latin scholarship and, *inter alia,* published in 1538 a translation of the whole of Lucian. In addition, it is only fair to rescue his personality from the *incognito* of " Micyllus " under which name, often misspelled, he usually appears, when cited. He owed this name to the fact that he took the rôle of the cobbler in a dramatization of Lucian's *Cock.*[109] " Micyllus," it may be noted, is the same impecunious cobbler who won publicity by his attempted exploit of swimming the River in his lack of ready money for Charon's fare.

Turning from the German Humanists to France, in the first half of the sixteenth century, we find an abundant menu of Lucianic suggestion and one less highly flavoured with theology.

Guillaume Budé (Budaeus),[110] the famous progenitor of the Collége de France and close contemporary of Erasmus, was inevitably inspired, by attending the lectures of Lascaris, who brought out the *editio princeps* of Lucian, to make his own translations from the Samosatan. These translations, together with those by Erasmus, were soon to be used by Rabelais.

At this period also, in the entourage of Margaret d'Angoulême, we find the witty Bonaventure Desperièrs pressing the Lucianic dialogue into the mould of the French vernacular which, as yet, was not entirely ready for the service.[111] His *Cymbalum Mundi* is a direct imitation of Lucian. This " is, in fact," Saintsbury observes, " one of the many proofs of the vast influence which Lucian exercised over the Renaissance." In his third dialogue, for example, the horse, able, by the intervention of Mercury, to hold a human conversation, reminds us of the Pythagoras-cock chatting with the cobbler and also endowed with the key to the situation by the kindness of the same god.

Just before the death of Erasmus the spirit of Lucianic mischief is reincarnated in Rabelais's more lusty *Pantagruel* and *Gargantua*. Grotesque as gargoyles his figures nevertheless, as Gildersleeve remarks,[112] are "Lucianic in outline." But though grotesque, Rabelais is not ill-proportioned. He is great in his grossness, his satire and imagination. The numerous comparisons of him with Lucian, Swift and Voltaire are instructive in so far as the critic is equipped with complete knowledge of all of them and is not deflected from objectivity by partisan preference. When dealing with great virility mere details of imitation concern us, perhaps, as little as the challenge of sources for Homer. An artist, however, may take details from more than one model. The extravaganza, for example, in Pantagruel (II, Chapt. xxx) is a clever *contaminatio* of Lucian's account in the *True Story*[113] and the closing scene in Plato's *Republic*. Epistemon's account of the Underworld, with its malicious list of certain eminent immigrants that he had met there, reminds us of how the souls in Plato's "Vision of Er" instead of always choosing lives similar to their former incarnations, in some cases perversely fly to the other extreme or to some travesty on their former state. So Rabelais's Helen is *courratière* (= *courtière*) *de chambrières;* Pope Alexander VI is a rat-catcher; pious Aeneas is a miller and shoulders a bag of meal as handily as if it were the aged Anchises; Commodus is a bag-piper; Darius, instead of cleaning up Greece, is set to a task resembling the fifth labour of Heracles, less imposing, indeed, but a permanent job! The grim democracy, however, and the compulsion are Lucianic enough. The poor have become great; Diogenes plays the grand prelate and lords it over Alexander; Epictetus invites Epistemon to a carousal. With this compare the item in Lucian's *True Story,* where Diogenes in Elysium "had so far changed his character as to marry the chummy Lais and would frequently, when in liquor, get up and dance and play drunken tricks."

Passing over numerous other contributors to the dialogue literature, especially in Germany, mentioned by Rentsch in his invaluable mono-

graph, we come to the charming Hans Sachs,
cobbler and mastersinger, who lived nearly a
quarter of a century longer than Rabelais. His
Latin source for Lucian seems to have been
the version by Vitus Bürler (1516). Though
a layman, Sachs could, on occasion, cobble a
Latin patch on his honest German sole-leather.
His omniverous appetite rejects nothing from
the Fall of Man to the contemporary theological pitfalls and, *inter alios,* he expressly names
Lucian with discriminating gusto among the
sources for his *Judicium Paridis:*

> *Homerus und Vergilius,*
> *Ovidius, Lucianus,*
> *Auch andre mehr gar Kunstenreich*
> *Doch in beschreybung ungeleich,*

and in the third act of this comedy Paris's appraisal of Juno has lost nothing of vividness in
his homely but vigorous German.

In *Die Himmelfahrt Margraff Albrechtz*
Hans Sachs transfers to *his* Charon the inexor-
able character of Lucian's Ferryman and his
relentless stripping of the proud and rich:
" Thou shalt not set foot in my boat," says
Charon to the Margraff, " till thou hast laid
aside all thy naughtiness and sins."

[154]

And, to take one more illustration, no debtor to Lucian's *True Story,* in all the goodly company from Rabelais to Baron Münchhausen, pays back a larger interest on his borrowed talents than does Hans Sachs in his quaint German description of his happy Schlaraffenland, where cooks would be but curious superfluities and where sturdy workmen solve the labor problem by dropping like ripe plums, not into the mouths of walking delegates, but each into a pair of working boots.

Before passing to writers, whose dates carry us over into the seventeenth century, mention may be made of the famous *Satyre Ménippée* which appeared in 1594. Apart from the title itself, in which the Lucianic tradition is patent, and beneath the specific allusions to Rabelais,[114] there might be found a diffused, if tacit, adaptation of Lucian's satire to the new journalism, so to say, of the time.

After the first decades of the sixteenth century not only was the Greek of Lucian accessible to scholars but Latin versions of a considerable part of his writings were at the disposal of all who could read Latin. " Quick and merrie dialogues, like those of Lucian " were included in the curriculum recommended

[155]

for the English school-boy of seven years of age. We are not told specifically whether these were in Greek, Latin, or English, but, at about this time, Lucian was filtering through the Latin into various vernaculars.[115]

Christopher Marlowe, whose untimely death in 1593 does not dissociate him from the group which binds the sixteenth and seventeenth centuries together, knew Lucian in Latin or Greek or both, and in his famous line on Helen: " Was this the face that launch'd a thousand ships? " recalls the cynical, but not wholly unsympathetic, remark of Menippus when Helen's skull is identified for him amongst other specimens in the chill museum of Hades: " Was it for this thing, then, that the thousand ships were manned from all Hellas? "

In this same group, for example, are Gabriel Harvey and Thomas Nashe whose mutual scurrilities were finally excluded from the market. They refer easily (if superficially) to Lucian in the frank amenities of their controversy. Thus Harvey, in *Foure Lectures* (1592), sums up an invective: " I overpasse Archilochus, Aristophanes, Lucian, Julian, Aretine and that whole venemous and viperous brood of old and new Raylers." In *Pierce's Supererogation*

(1593) he diagnoses Nashe's writings: "As true, peradventure, as Lucian's *true, narrations* or the heroicall historyes of Rabelais," etc. etc. Nashe replied with appropriate sentiments. Incidently, it may be noted, Nashe refers to the *Syrian Goddess* (a piece not often cited), which he had evidently read in the *verse* translation. In *Anatomie of Absurdity* (1589), defending fiction, he says: " In his books *De Siria Dea* " . . . " Lucian an Heathen Poet wrote of that universall flood that was in the time of Noe."

Thomas Dekker and Ben Jonson, close contemporaries (1570/1573 to 1637), and, on occasion, ardent adversaries, used Lucian freely. Dekker, for example, in *the Devil let loose with his Anfwere to Pierce Pennylesse*, borrowed with both hands from Lucian's fourth *Dialogue of the Dead*, and, as has been suggested,[116] had also " certainly read the *Menippus* of Lucian in John Rastell's translation and travestied it in his own fashion in his *News from Hell*."

Ben Jonson's reminiscences of Lucian are numerous. *Poetaster*, for example, Act. IV, Scene 5, is based on Lucian's *Lexiphanes*. Dekker noticed this and in his *Satiromastix*, Act

IV, Scene 2, makes his "Tucca" call the "Horace (-Jonson)" by the name of "Lucian." This also indicates the contemporary pervasiveness of the Samosatan. Scene 5 of Act IV is more or less directly reminiscent of Lucian's *Assembly of the Gods,* and "the fundamental situation in the *Silent Woman,*" as has been pointed out,[117] "is Lucianic." *Volpone,* an unrestrained satire on legacy hunters, draws freely from this motif in Lucian's *Dialogues of the Dead* — and, still more to the point, specifically mentions Lucian's *Cock* as model for this racy dialogue where [118] "Androgyno" gives the vital statistics of the transmigrations of his soul from Apollo, via Pythagoras, to his present hermaphroditic hostelry.

A tabulation, in parallel columns, of *Volpone* and the *Cock* would show that Ben Jonson, while injecting new quips with coarser wit, has closely followed the framework in Lucian.

Beaumont, Cervantes and Shakespeare all died in 1616. (Beaumont and) Fletcher's [119] *Four Plays or Moral Representations in One* closes with the *Triumph of Time.* This is clearly modelled on Lucian's *Timon* and retains the Aristophanic epiphany of the god

Plutus, a vital prelude which is wholly lacking
in " Shakespeare's " *Timon of Athens*. The
little drama closes leaving Anthropos (=
" Everyman ") famed for his wealth and with
" Labour " also as his companion — a very
moral though bouleversant addition. The type
of Misanthrope is not preserved.

For Shakespeare's use of Lucian, either
through a Latin or an English version, we
now [120] have a sufficiently convincing argument, not only for *Timon of Athens*, of probably composite [121] authorship, but, more to the
point, for the " Grave-scene of Hamlet."

In the introduction to *Don Quixote* Cervantes gives a nearer parallel to Lucian's *How
to Write History* and to the opening of the
True Story than he does in the body of the
work itself, with its special crusade against a
creed of chivalry outworn, but even here we
feel the Lucianic touch in the esoteric satire
directed against braggarts and liars. We must,
however, repeatedly adjust ourselves to the
broadly farcical, whereas in Lucian's *True
Story* all doubts and probabilities alike drop
out of sight when once we have cleared the
Pillars of Heracles.

Que Vedo, the brilliant compatriot and

younger contemporary of Cervantes, cuts many
a sharp Lucianic silhouette, reminiscent of the
Dialogues of the Dead, in his *Visions* (Sueños),
published in 1627 — *e.g.,* the death-dealing
physicians; the judges with deaf ears and re-
ceptive hands; the poets condemned in the
Underworld to correct the poems of rivals;
Solon as *post mortem* prosecutor of tyrants,
from Pisistratus to Caligula.[122] There are also
various less obvious reminiscences of the *True
Story.*

In France Cyrano de Bergerac, a little later,
continued the vogue of the *True Story* in his
two posthumous pieces: *Histoire comique des
états et empires de la lune* (1656) and *du
soleil* (1661). In addition to the reminiscences
of Lucian's *True Story* in the *Voyage to the
Moon* the parallels with the *Icaromenippus* are
equally suggestive. For example, Cyrano's
" Demon " of Socrates reminds us of the apparition of Empedocles in *Icaromenippus;* so,
too, Cyrano's return to the earth in the arms
of the " Demon " seems like a combination of
Icaromenippus's trip to heaven in his flying-
machine and his return trip, with Hermes
holding him by the ear! Cyrano's view of the
outspread world recalls Lucian's love for

aërial panoramas, as in the *Icaromenippus,
Twice Accused, Charon* and *The Runaways*.
Among the occasional close reproductions may
be cited Cyrano's *Lychnobii,* as suggested by
the *Lychnopolis* of the *True Story.*

Molière, as we are told, spent five years in
company with Cyrano de Bergerac and it
would not be surprising to identify in him also
some loan material from Lucian, incorporated
as nonchalantly as his loot from Lucretius.
In *Le Misanthrope,* however, where one might
naturally look for reminiscence, the type set
by Lucian in his *Timon* is so overlaid with the
peevishness of the jealous lover that it emerges
only dimly at the end of the play.

To attribute to the eagle intellect of Pascal,
close contemporary of Molière and Cyrano, indebtedness to Lucian would be far-fetched.
Nevertheless no better parallel could be found
for an intimate appraisal of Lucian's attitude
towards the Stoic and Epicurean Schools of
philosophy than Pascal's chapter *Sur Épictète
et Montaigne.* It solves, so far as is possible,
the *impasse,* to which we are brought at the
end of the *Hermotimus,* Lucian's would-be
magnum opus. It repeats Lucian's open mockery, in the *Sale of Soul Samples,* of the scep-

tic's equally balanced scales, yet explains how
Lucian could find shelter for his own deep-
dyed scepticism under the robe of the Epicurean. And, in this connection, it may be noted
that no one of the modern imitations of Lucian's *Dialogues of the Dead* is more successful than Traill's dialogue between *Pascal and
Lucian* in his *New Lucian.*

Hickes's admirable translations from Lucian into English were published in 1634.
These were almost certainly *not* the first, but
from this time on Lucian was accessible in the
English vernacular and it is a temptation, here
and there, to identify as a far-flung ripple of
his influence what may be of quite independent
origin. As to Butler's *Hudibras,* for example,
it is safe to content ourselves with Saintsbury's [123] juxtaposition of Lucian, Butler and
the authors of the *Satire Ménippée* as being
alike unrivalled in the adroitness with which
they cause their characters to make themselves
ridiculous. Such similarity in talent does not
prove indebtedness.

In the foreshortened perspective of the centuries we get the impression of a long, almost
unbroken,[124] procession of writers who have
made more or less use of Lucian's *Dialogues of*

the Dead. Many of these make use of the form only. Some " take the chaff and let the grain lie still." But with some, as notably Erasmus, the grain fructifies.

Matthew Prior (1664–1672), in his four dialogues of worthy (or unworthy) dead men, makes his own stimulating contribution. His sarcasm on the futilities of philosophy, in the person of Locke, is as superficial as Lucian's own contempt for the exhibits of the " Human Understanding " in his day, though he plays with Montaigne's formula — " Que sais-je? " — with more objectivity than was usual with Lucian, the more serious missionary agnostic. Cromwell, too, with the help of his " porter," lays bare, quite in accord with Lucian's method, his own arrogance and greed of power, sheltered within his exterior pomp. Prior, however, as is, indeed, the general rule with those who make use of this literary form, fails to avail himself of a device characteristic of Lucian's dialogues. The introduction, usual in Lucian's *dramatis personae,* of some member of the permanent staff — like Aeacus, Clotho, Hermes or Pluto — gave a dramatic vividness and finish that we miss in the society of merely disinterred humans.

"Dryden's" *Lucian* [125] is a different matter.
The translation was not completed until after
his death. He did not know the qualifications,
nor even the names, of all the large number of
translators, some of them very raw recruits,
that were afterwards mustered in to fill up
his skeleton company. His own contribution
was the *Life of Lucian* which appears in Dryden's collected works. This demands mention
here because the author's fame might still give
currency to his banal misinterpretations of the
formidable array of errors which he has managed to accumulate at second-hand. Dryden
has no sense of perspective for Lucian's times,
and the subtler ironies seem to escape him
altogether. His preachments on Christianity
and morality are on a par with his introduction
to his translation of Juvenal whose blast-fur-
nace he heats, with lascivious enthusiasm,
seven times hotter than the Roman satirist was
wont to heat it. It was fortunate for Lucian
that Dryden, whether by the timely arrival of
Death or by a lurking consciousness of his own
inadequate acquaintance with the original, was
restrained from translating himself the half-
dozen, or fewer, passages in all Lucian's voluminous writings which might have given him

another thin but convenient smoke-screen for expansive wantonness.

The vogue for the dialogue in England towards the end of the seventeenth century is repeated in France. Boileau gave impetus to imitations of Lucian by his *Dialogue à la manière de Lucien: les Héros de roman.* Although the authorized publication of this was delayed till 1713, it had been privately recited much earlier and surreptitious, printed use of it had been made from memory by one of his hearers. This dialogue is no mere imitation of the *Dialogues of the Dead.* It has its own originality and is Lucianic in a wider sense. It is from the *True Story* that Boileau borrows the suggestion for the rebellion of the damned, but this satire directed against the pseudo-heroes has more of the flavour of Lucian's account, in his *Fisher,* of the false philosophers and his summary treatment of the queer fish. Not every glittering goldfish is a Chrysippus, and Boileau's pseudo-heroes are stripped as naked as Lucian's dead and driven forth to punishment. Or, again, in the *Fragment d'un dialogue* where Boileau picks flaws in Horace's bad French, — an inverted criticism on the bad Latin of French poetasters, —

we think of Lucian's crusade in his *Lexiphanes* against the would-be Atticists of his day.

Fontenelle's *Dialogues des Morts* were published in 1683, dedicated: " À Lucien, aux champs Élysiens." In acknowledging his debt he is somewhat wooden and self-depreciatory but the dialogues themselves contain many a worthy touch, *e.g.* in his *Charles V et Érasme,* where Erasmus triumphs over the emperor, now " in reduced circumstances," only to be blighted presently by the discovery that to have been born " avec un cerveau bien disposé " is just as unmarketable an asset in the " champs Élysiens " as to have had " un père qui soit roi." Thus Fontenelle outdoes Lucian's own withering *égalité* in Hades.

His juxtaposition of the protagonists in his dialogues is amusing enough. In Lucian's famous dialogue where Alexander the Great contends with Scipio and Hannibal for the hegemony there could be no doubt about the verdict, but in Fontenelle Alexander finds himself pitted against a greater and more invincible conqueror, the famous Phryne! Or Dido complains to her confidante because Virgil has spoiled her reputation by a wholly unsatisfactory and anachronistic affair with a passé lover some two hundred and fifty years her senior. Or, again, the shade of the Greek physician, Erasistratus, has new blood pumped into his vacant veins by Dr. Harvey! All this is amusing enough but we are not always conscious, as we are in Lucian, of the grim verities of Pluto's realm. "Not seldom we feel," as Rentsch acutely observes,[126] "that these conversations could just as well have taken place in a Paris salon." Even in his *Jugement de Pluton*, with Hades in the title-rôle, Fontenelle still keeps one foot in the world above when the *ante mortem* trial of his own book takes place in the underworld, with Lucian himself acting as proxy and advocate for the author.

Le Sage early in the eighteenth century embodies in his famous novels suggestions of Lucian's influence, derived indirectly, perhaps, through Spanish and Italian intermediaries. In *Le Diable Boiteaux* he makes use [127] of the cock's tail-feather as a magic key, just as Lucian does, and reminds us also of the satire on magic in the *Lie-Fancier*. In this novel and in *Une Journée des Parques*, characterized by Saintsbury as "a keen piece of Lucianic satire," the debt, such as it is, involved specifically the satiric element but in his great

[167]

novel *Gil Blas* it is the skill in narrative and
incidents that recalls the *True Story* and, possibly through Cervantes, the *Asinus* of Lucian.

While Fontenelle, in the rapidly swelling
flood of imitators of the *Dialogues of the Dead,*
had used the form largely to introduce amusing
conversations, his compatriot Fénelon made
use of it often with a more serious purpose.
One example must suffice. In his admirable
dialogue (No. xv), *Herodote et Lucien,* the
Father of History wishes that Lucian, by way
of punishment for his superficial raillery, might
be forced, in a new reincarnation, to go over
Herodotus's itinerary and so verify the truth
of all his statements. Lucian, expanding the
idea to take in all his criticisms of life, coun-
ters, in good French: " Cela seroit bien joli.
I should then," he continues, " pass from body
to body through all the sects of the philosophers whom I have derided. Thus I should
come to hold, one after another, all the mutually exclusive opinions that I have mocked."
This is the very essence of the situation at the
end of the *Hermotimus*. But Fénelon, although
he reproduces more vividly than Fontenelle
this serious side of their common model, does
not rest in Lucian's negative pessimism. Eu-

[168]

ropean ethics in statesmanship, or in daily life, are illustrated by Lucianic parallels and wholesomely castigated. For the years immediately preceding Fénelon these dialogues of his might well be used in adjusting the perspective of history.

Nor does Fénelon fail to note the more characteristic humour of the original. Nothing, perhaps, in Lucian is neater than the metaphysical and yet severely biological explanation by Heracles of his dual *post mortem* assets. He stoutly maintains that the Heracles in heaven, enjoying conjugal bliss with Hebe, is one and the same, through all eternity, with the desiccated and lonely shade of Heracles in Hades! Fénelon includes this quip also in his second dialogue. Another choice Lucianic scene is recalled, not taken from the *Dialogues of the Dead* but staged by Lucian in the Afterworld in his *True History,* where young Cinyras elopes from heaven with Helen, " das ewig Weibliche." So Fénelon, in No. xx, reveals an intrigue between Alcibiades and Proserpine.

In 1726/7 *Gulliver's Travels* appeared. Swift was openly indebted [128] to Rabelais and, like Fontenelle, borrowed hints, here and there, from Cyrano de Bergerac. In various matters, however, like the interviewing of Homer and Aristotle with their commentators, and still more perhaps in the air of verisimilitude of the details, with which he surrounds the impossible, we may recognize a more direct influence of Lucian's *True Story*.

Of all the expert critics who venture detailed comparison of the four great writers inevitably brought into juxtaposition M. Maurice Croiset, perhaps, is best entitled to speak with authority. After brief but incisive words on his own compatriots, Rabelais and Voltaire, he renders [129] this quite objective verdict: " Swift est peut-être celui qui ressemble le plus à Lucien. . . . Seulement l'écrivain anglais a plus de flegme et de parti pris; il y a quelque chose de plus voulu dans sa fantaisie, et par suite elle a moins de charme et variété." Swift's bitter satire, we may add, recalls Juvenal rather than the more genial humour of Lucian, if we except the latter's more frankly polemical writings, like *Alexander the Fake-Prophet*.

Ludwig von Holberg, the Norwegian " founder " of Danish literature, following in Swift's wake, published first in Latin and then in Danish, in 1727, *Nicolai Klimii Iter Subterraneum*,

a legatee of Lucian's *True Story* and, by its
very title, a forerunner of Jules Verne in his
Voyage au centre de la terre. This fantasy not
only gained instant popularity in Denmark but
was widely translated from the Latin edition
into the other languages.[130] When compared
with Lucian, Swift, or other narrators of the
impossible, it is not surprising that this work
has failed to maintain its hold on readers. The
marvels are not introduced with a humour
sufficiently light and plausible to counteract
irritation. The didactic application of the
bouleversed "subterraneous" conditions to
Holberg's contemporary world grows wearisome. Occasionally there is a happy turn. All
the inhabitants of the miniature continent below are trees walking like men. When Klim
effects his first landing he is attacked by a bull
and seeks refuge in the bosom of the nearest
tree whose sex and kinetic abilities he has not
yet noticed. He receives a sudden box on the
ear from an upper limb and is forthwith haled
into court for taking liberties with the wife
of the High Sheriff! But these human trees are
too much with us and remain very naturally
wooden.

In eighteenth-century Germany, amazing use

of Lucian's *Dialogues of the Dead* was made
by feeding imitations of them into the hopper
of periodic journalism. This was as remarkable
for its banality as for its volume. One example
will suffice. A certain David Fassmann, beginning in 1718, published in Leipzig for twenty-
two years a monthly periodical containing dialogues between dead men, distinguished and
otherwise. These issues mounted up to more
than 20,000 pages! That Lucian's influence
could survive this wide-spread and long-con-
tinued abuse of his legacy is, incidentally, another proof of his vitality.

Voltaire lived from 1694–1778. His obligations to Lucian and certain parallels between
their lives are obvious enough. Lucian has been
loosely called the Voltaire of the second century and Voltaire the Lucian of the eighteenth.
But the complexity of human life in the inter-
val had increased too much for such designa-
tions to be convertible. A more accurate diagnosis is demanded and has repeatedly been
made by competent critics.[131] Since the middle
of the nineteenth century it is possible to accord
to Voltaire much fairer criticism than the preju-
diced abuse which he himself, for example, be-
stowed upon Rabelais. He is no longer disposed

of as merely a nihilistic sceptic. Lucian's destructive criticism is more thoroughgoing. Voltaire, however, is still more remote from Erasmus, who is the best interpreter of Lucian's
best work and able, with his more optimistic
humanism, to counteract the poison of pessimism while, at the same time, he adapts to
the needs of his own day the wholesome, if
bitter, satire of the Greek iconoclast. Voltaire's
" sniggering and semi-virile indecency," however, — to quote Mr. Saintsbury's somewhat
caustic phrase [132] — does not prevent the vivid
use, especially in his dialogues, of as much of
Lucian's spirit as he had chosen to understand.

His dialogue, *Lucien, Érasme et Rabelais*,[133]
gives good illustration. In this Voltaire himself
masquerades under the guise of Erasmus. The
three have rendezvous, presumably in Hades.
Lucian informs himself as to the vital statistics
of his two distinguished " epigoni " and then
sits down to read presentation copies of their
works in order to bring himself up to date. In
the end all three go off in company with the
newly-arrived Dean Swift. The " big four "
have formed a syndicate with Voltaire as
General Manager.

Apart from the dialogues, Lucian's *True*

Story is reflected in *Micromégas* and in *Candide*. In *Candide* also we get an echo of the *Hermotimus*, and Lucian's paralyzing agnosticism in the conclusion of this dialogue has reenforcement in Voltaire's *Gallimatias Dramatique*, where the Chinese refuse to give heed to the ex parte preaching of Jesuit or Jansenist, Puritan, Quaker, Anglican, Lutheran, Mussulman or Jew.

The *Dialogues of the Dead* by George Lord Lyttleton (1760) are specifically modelled upon Lucian, Fénelon and Fontenelle. They have, however, their own distinction and originality. The author takes antiquity and himself with naïve seriousness. He explains his method in detail and prides himself upon his intelligence in selecting his interlocutors wholly from those who are no longer living. He is at pains to defend himself against any possible charge of paganism in introducing Elysium, Minos, Mercury, Charon and Styx, which are, as he observes, " necessary Allegories in this way of writing " and not the underlying beliefs of a " catholic mind!" Without clearly realizing it, he thus retains, on occasion, though imperfectly, one of Lucian's most important artistic devices. For example, Addison and Swift refer the question of precedence to Mercury. Mercury, too, has to intervene in a violent quarrel between a deceased North American savage and an English duellist. The savage, like the cobbler in Lucian, starts to swim across the Styx not, however, because he cannot pay the fare, but because he is unwilling to set foot in the same boat with the immoral duellist!

The last dialogue, *Plutarch — Charon — and a modern Bookseller,* is one of three written by an anonymous friend and, as a Lucianic dialogue, is the best in the collection. The bookseller furnishes an amusing pendant to the stock character of the " tyrant " in Lucian who tries to beg off from punishment.

Friederich Earle Raspe published (1785), in English, *Baron Münchhausen's Narrative of his Marvellous Travels and Campaigns in Russia*. In this famous work we find undisguised, sometimes almost *verbatim*, imitations of Lucian's still germinant narrative in the *True Story*.[134]

Of the great German group, overlapping into the nineteenth century, Lessing knew Lucian, but evidently found him little akin to his serious purposes.[135]

Wieland, the famous translator of Lucian at

the end of the eighteenth century, essayed also
to imitate his favourite author in his *Gespräche
in Élysium* and is reminiscent of him in his romance *Don Sylvio von Rosalva* written in the
manner of *Don Quixote.* Precisely, however,
in connection with Lucian he calls down on his
own head the irony and satire of his two greater
compatriots and successors.

Schiller in his distichs [136] — suggestive also
of the *Hermotimus* — has a meeting between
Lucian and Wieland who had tried to white-
wash the cynic Peregrinus Proteus. Peregrinus, in fact, sends up word to Wieland that
this is love's labour lost: " ich war doch ein
Lump!" — and when Wieland asks Lucian
whether he is now reconciled with the philosophers, Schiller makes Lucian's corpse reply
somewhat ironically: " Softly, my friend!
While I was chastising the fools I have often
plagued also the wise! "

Goethe's attack on Wieland is over-bitter in
his farce, *Götter, Helden und Wieland,* but he
shows, incidentally, his insight into Lucianic
satire. His Hercules, for example, is a replica
of Lucian's Heracles in the sixteenth *Dialogue
of the Dead;* and Lucian as well as Aeschylus
might, perhaps, be traced in the acrid lines of

Goethe's *Prometheus,* and still more confidently may we catch in Faust's pessimistic monologue the despair of the disillusioned Stoic neophyte, Hermotimus.

And, again, a tale in Lucian's *Lie-Fancier* is openly reproduced by Goethe in his witty poem, *Der Zauberlehrling* where the Magician's Prentice by means of the magic formula turns the broom — (instead of the Lucianic pestle or bar of the door — an unessential variant) — into an efficient body-servant. The outcome in both versions is the same. The Rev. Richard Barham, however, Goethe's junior by some forty years, makes two innovations in his rollicking *Lay of St. Dunstan.* He substitutes, as in Goethe, a broom-stick for the bar or pestle and, as in the other two versions, the broom, or bar, is cut in two by the frightened tyro in magic who has failed to secure the second formula which will cause the over-organized valet to revert again to inorganic matter. The two halves now bring twice as fast what was ordered. In Lucian and Goethe the order was for water and the Master in each case arrives just in time to save the pupil from drowning. The Reverend Mr. Barham, however, less temperate than the Greek or German,

changes water into wine and causes " Peter the
Lay Brother " to order up such unlimited
drinks that a tragedy results. He is unequal
to the supply and is drowned before he can be
rescued from the officious bar-tenders.

In Lucian's *Menippus* or *Necromancy,* we
are told that our shadows, inseparable com-
panions during life and therefore well-informed
about all our doings, testify against us after
death. This idea, which may go back to Lucretius,[137] is skilfully inverted by von Chamisso in *Peter Schlemihl's Wunderbare Ge-
schichte* (1814), or, "The Man Without a
Shadow." [138] And E. T. A. Hoffman, *Die Ge-
schichte vom verlorenen Spiegelbilde* (1815),
developed this conceit by causing one of his
heroes to sign away his mirror reflection, thus
putting him in much the same class with Peter
Schlemihl.

Turning again to England we may mention,
in addition to Barham, the following sample
reminders of Lucian in the first half of the
nineteenth century. The *Imaginary Conversations* of Walter Savage Landor, enlarged to six
volumes during some thirty years of his long,
ebullient life, reproduce too many phases of
human experience to be described under any

one rubric. Parallel lives, or deaths for that
matter, reflect Plutarch. Herodotus, the dra-
matists and Plato furnish points of departure;
but Landor's self dominates the matter. It is
not, however, mere fancy to feel Lucian's spirit
in the polemic dialogues, and the actual conversation between *Lucian and Timotheus* is
Lucian to the life — sealed, signed and delivered. It is not reminiscent of the *Dialogues of
the Dead* so much as it is of the destructive
method of the *Hermotimus*, albeit the slippery
and sloppy ecclesiastic, Timotheus, is too im-
pervious to logic to realize, as does the Stoic
undergraduate at the end of Lucian's dialogue,
that he has no position remaining — not even
a mathematical point. Unlike Erasmus, Landor
is not careful to temper Lucian's bitterness and
gives himself up to unreasoned prejudice more
often than did Lucian himself.

The juxtaposition of Thomas L. Beddoes and
Lucian must be more tentative as there is no
open reference to Lucian. The rejected title,
however, for *Death's Jest Book*, "Charonic
Steps," found in the MS. of 1832, would have
been a near-Lucian signature. Even his detailed delight in the pageantry of Death, in
"the swift, theatrical transitions"[139] that at-

tend the transfer of monarchs to the democracy of Hades, need not, of course, come from his familiarity with Lucian. And the vivid " Dance of Death " in *Death's Jest Book* may be only one more reminder of this motif, so wide-spread in mediaeval art.

For the reminiscences in the nineteenth century,[140] the following names may serve to indicate, though in different ways and in varying degrees, the persistence of the literary tradition.

Edward Bulwer Lytton published *The New Timon* anonymously in 1847, the year that Beddoes died. This melodramatic novel in verse has nothing in common with Lucian, apart from the title, and his misanthrope is a vague distortion of the accepted type. More reminiscent of Lucian in his *True Story* is the story of the subterranean realm, entitled *The Coming Race*. This highly imaginative work reëchoes Holberg's *Iter Subterraneum*, to which it is much superior, though in its didactic seriousness it lacks utterly the humour of Lucian's fantasies.

Robert Browning, in his poem *Pheidippides,* perpetuates a mistake made by Lucian himself, who confuses [141] the Herodotean courier be-

tween Athens and Sparta with the soldier
Eucles, or Thersippus, who ran in full armour,
after the battle, from Marathon to Athens.
Plutarch had recorded the story in *De Gloria
Atheniensium* but Lucian chose to ignore, or
was actually ignorant of, his account. Browning's mind was richly furnished with Greek literature, Lucian included. In *Pippa Passes:*[142]

> As *some Greek dog-sage, dead and merry,*
> Hellward *bound in Charon's wherry*

is a snap-shot of the Cynic, Menippus, *en voyage.* Browning would not have balked at the
anachronism of translating the title, *Cataplus,*
as the *Hellbent Voyage.*

James Anthony Froude was, as might be ex-
pected, an eager and sympathetic interpreter of
Lucian to the nineteenth century. He includes
Lucian among his *Short Studies on Great Sub-
jects* [143] and his occasional inaccuracies, due to
a jaunty reliance on his memory, do not seri-
ously detract from the value of his vivid sketch.
These, indeed, are forgotten in the verve with
which he translates part of the *Tragical Zeus.*
His summation (p. 214), finally, is noteworthy:
" Lucian more than any other writer, pagan or
Christian, enables us to see what human beings

were, how they lived, what they thought, felt, said and did in the centuries when paganism was expiring and Christianity was taking its place."

Jules Verne published in 1864 his *Voyage au centre de la terre,* and in 1865 *De la terre à la lune.* Although it is a far cry from the nineteenth to the second century, there seems to be no reason to differ from the usual opinion that traces back the inventions of his fantasy through *Cyrano de Bergerac* in the seventeenth century, via, perhaps, the *Iter Subterraneum* of Holberg in the eighteenth, to the *True Story* and *Icaromenippus* of Lucian.

Walter Pater's chapter, in *Marius the Epicurean,* entitled " A Conversation Not Imaginary," is worth a whole volume of " Imaginary Conversations," so far as an actual appraisal of Lucian is concerned. Pater, in his own brilliant way, works into this chapter the content of the *Hermotimus* which, although imitated less continuously through the centuries than the *Dialogues of the Dead* and the *True Story,* has been again and again a stimulant to our author's more thoughtful readers. One rather violent change is made by Pater in Lucian's *dramatis personae.* Lucian's sixty-year-old

Stoic undergraduate, who has barely reached the foot-hills of the steep height of Virtue, is turned into an eager beginner in his early youth. This alters the perspective materially but it is done for artistic reasons and we cannot quarrel with the result in Pater's exquisite setting.

To turn to Andrew Lang's *Letters to Dead Authors,* ranging, more widely than Petrarch's,[144] from Homer to Pepys, is to raise the curtain and to watch across the brilliant footlights of his *facetiae* the entrances and all too sudden exits of dead actors who still take their unerring cues from life. Into the seven brief pages devoted to " Lucian of Samosata " Lang compacts more that is vital to an understanding of Lucian, more that recalls, to those who already know him well, the versatility of his fantasy than seems credible in so small a compass. Incidentally, the parody on the *Sale of Soul Samples* is so perfect that one grieves to think that Lucian himself, on receipt of the letter, must fail, from ignorance of the world of to-day, to detect all the nuances of delicate satire.

The literary device of *Dialogues of the Dead,* " that maintained its popularity from Lucian down to Lyttleton, and from Lyttleton up to

Landor," [145] reappears in altered and much ex-
panded form in the three hundred pages of
Marion Crawford's *With the Immortals,* but
Lucian's ghost gives forth no whisper at the
behest of the cold-storage battery installed by
Crawford in the outraged Mediterranean. The
nearest reminder is the immortal ghost of
Heine, happily selected by Crawford as pro-
tagonist.

The New Lucian, by Henry D. Traill,[146] re-
habilitates with vigour and wit the often ill-
used *Dialogues of the Dead.* The dialogue between *Lucian and Pascal,* so happily paired, is
a special contribution to Lucianic study.

Lucian, finally, is not wholly forgotten, even
in this industrial twentieth century. Fridtjof
Nansen's *In Northern Mists* (1911) is the
work of a scholar as well as a famous explorer.
The very frequent use that he makes of Lucian's *True Story,* along with other Greek
sources, from the *Odyssey* on, reënforces our
conception of Lucian's influence, aside from
his familiar place in literature, as an active element through oral tradition in the extension,
if not the creation, of popular beliefs concerning the uncharted mysteries of the physical
world.

[184]

Especially in Chapter IX, entitled "Wine-land the Good," Nansen's metamorphosis of the "Islands of the Blest" and the "Elysian Fields," etc., into the derivative Germanic Schlaraffenland, and other congeners, is at once a stimulating study in comparative Irish and Scandinavian folk-lore and, what is more to our purpose, furnishes copious parallels for Lucian's *True Story*. These details are so numerous and so striking that Nansen concludes: "It looks as if Lucian's stories had reached Ireland (*e.g.*, by Scandinavian travellers or through Arabs?) long before the *Navigatio Brandani* was written." [147] If Nansen is right Lucian in the underworld must often have been vexed at having his fantasy thus turned into fact!

Further details might be mentioned. Nansen, in his subsequent volume,[148] draws a parallel between the fabulous chasm — the Norse "Ginnungagap" — and Lucian's most unbridled flight of fancy when his ship, in the *True Story*, comes suddenly upon the one-thousand-furlong-deep chasm of air dividing the sea.

A nobler work by Lucian, *The Charon*, is also cited by Nansen, with parallels from the Norse and Germanic tradition, for the essential

idea of the "Ferry of Death." But the vari-
ants are as striking as the resemblances — the
Scandinavian Acheron and Styx are as wide as
the North Sea!

As tail-piece to this first quarter of the twentieth century, we may close with a reference to
the *Lucianic Dialogue between Socrates in
Hades and Certain Men of the Present Day*,
by W. F. R. Hardie.[149] This is written in Greek
more academically flawless than Lucian's. Here
De Valera comes off badly when he tries to ex-
plain to Socrates his notion of " freedom, free
to slay herself." Lloyd George has his attention called to his inconsistency in " black-
guarding landholders, though a farmer himself ":

$$\tau o\dot{\upsilon}\varsigma \ \gamma\hat{\eta}\nu \ \ddot{\epsilon}\chi o\nu\tau\alpha\varsigma \ \lambda o\iota\delta o\rho\hat{\omega} \ \gamma\epsilon\omega\rho\gamma\dot{o}\varsigma \ \ddot{\omega}\nu.$$

A Coué patient, like an aspiring horse walking
the rollers of an old-time threshing machine,
repeats his formula: " I'm growing better every
day,"

$$\alpha i\dot{\epsilon}\nu \ \beta\epsilon\lambda\tau\dot{\iota}\omega\nu, \ \beta\epsilon\lambda\tau\dot{\iota}\omega\nu \ \alpha i\dot{\epsilon}\nu \ \dot{\epsilon}\mu\alpha\upsilon\tauο\hat{\upsilon}$$
$$\sigma\hat{\omega}\mu\dot{\alpha} \ \tau\epsilon \ \kappa\alpha i \ \psi\upsilon\chi\dot{\eta}\nu \ \epsilon i\mu\iota \ \kappa\alpha\tau' \ \hat{\eta}\mu\alpha\rho \ \dot{\epsilon}\gamma\dot{\omega},$$

as well he might if he could write such good
Greek or would read attentively Lucian's *Lie-*

Fancier! Satire is still as sanatory in the twentieth as in the second century. As a part of our " Debt to Greece " it also, like Kipling's *Banjo,* draws

> . . . . . *the world together, link by link:*
> *Yea, from Delos up to Limerick and back!*

NOTES AND BIBLIOGRAPHY

NOTES

Grateful acknowledgment of indebtedness for various helpful references is made to Dr. G. Alder Blumer; to Professors J. C. Adams of Yale, Jos. Jastrow of Wisconsin, A. Trowbridge of Princeton; to Director L. E. Rowe of the R. I. School of Design; to the author's colleagues: Professors Clough, Crowell, Hastings, Koopman, and R. M. Mitchell; and also to Professor G. H. Chase and the Fogg Museum, Harvard, and Director B. H. Hill of Athens and the Boston Museum of Fine Arts for their courtesies in obtaining the illustrations. Also to Messrs. Ginn and Co. for permission to use matter in Allinson's *Lucian* (College Series of Greek Authors).

1. For a different emphasis see the able article " Lucian the Sophist," by Emily J. Putnam, in *Classical Philology*, iv. 162–177 (1909).

2. Cf. M. Croiset, *La Vie et les Oeuvres de Lucien,* Paris, 1882, p. 390.

3. *Op. cit.,* p. 393. For detailed illustration of Lucian's influence see below, Chapter VIII, pp. 130–187.

4. Cf. A. D. Fraser, " The Age of the Extant Columns of the Olympieium at Athens," in *Art Bulletin,* iv. (1921). The temple, newly oriented on the Pisistratus site, was begun by Antiochus Epiphanes but left unfinished at his death in 164 B.C. and finished and dedicated by Hadrian in 131 A.D.

5. Only as a *very* recherché piece of satire could this be assigned to Lucian.

6. Cf. Franz Cumont, *After Life in Roman Paganism,* New Haven and London, 1922, p. 17 *et passim.* See, also, his *Astrology and Religion among the Greeks and Romans,* New York and London, 1912, p. 53: " It is to their (*i.e.,* the Greeks') everlasting honour that, amid the tangle of precise observations and superstitious fancies which made

up the priestly lore of the East, they discovered and utilised the serious elements, while neglecting the rubbish."

7. For such an imaginary banquet at the villa of Atticus, see *Roads from Rome*, A. C. E. Allinson, New York, 1922, pp. 194–215.

8. See Suidas, article Λουκιανός; Photius, *Biblioth.* 128; Lactantius, *Inst. div.*, I. 9; Eunapius, *Lives of the Philosophers*, preface — cited and discussed by Croiset, *op. cit.*, Chapter I.

9. Or by 117 A.D. if born under the Emperor Trajan as Suidas vaguely asserts. Croiset, *op. cit.*, pp. 2 and 52, argues for 125 A.D.

10. Harmon's rendering. (See Bibliography.)

11. *Pro Lapsu in Salutando*, 13. For Lucian's actual citation or reminiscences of Latin authors, see below, p. 125 (Chapter VIII).

12. See B. L. Gildersleeve, *Essays and Studies*, Baltimore, 1890, p. 108, on Lucian's *Complete Rhetorician*.

13. If we include *Asinus, Suit of Sigma against Tau,* and the *Syrian Goddess.*

14. Text and translation in *The Loeb Classical Library* (by A. M. Harmon) will occupy eight vols. when completed.

15. M. Croiset (*op. cit.*), decides tentatively for 4 or 5 periods: (a) Works written before Lucian's " conversion " from Rhetoric; (b) His first essays in a new *genre* — under the influence of Middle and New Comedy; (b. 2) The large Menippean group; (c) Maturer products under influence of Old Comedy; (d) Writings of his old age. More arbitrary is the chronological arrangement of P. M. Bolderman, *Studia Lucianea*, Leyden, 1898: (1) Those before 155 A.D.; (2) From 155–165 A.D.; (3) From 165–180 A.D.; (4) After 180 A.D. This is usefully concrete.

16. *Vera Historia*, II. 21.

17. *Icaromenippus*, 18.

18. *Dial. Mort.*, 21.

19. Juvenal, *Sat.*, II. 4:

　　. . . . . *quamquam plena omnia gypso*
　　Chrysippi invenias.

20. *Apologia*, 15. Rohde (see Bibliography), p. 324.

21. See *Icaromenippus*, 13.

22. Erasmus, for example, see below, page 147.

23. B. L. Gildersleeve, *op. cit.*, p. 351.

24. *Epitrepontes*, 179K, F. G. Allinson in *The Loeb Classical Library*, p. 126.

25. Cf. Franz Cumont, *op. cit.*, p. 39.

26. See *Peregrinus*, 11–13.

27. *Cataplus* or " The Voyage Down."

28. Interlocutor also in the *Cock,* see below, p. 101. For his literary immortality, see below, p. 150.

29. Franz Cumont (*op. cit.*, p. 106), compares Lucian's journey to heaven with " the three stages " of the journey to Paradise " widely entertained in the East." He adds: " A trace of this belief seems to linger " in Saint Paul's reference to being " lifted to the third heaven " (2 *Corinth.*, 12, 2). For the hero carried up to heaven by an eagle in the Persian epic of Firdausi, " an ancestor probably of the eagle in Chaucer's *House of Fame,*" see W. P. Ker, *The Dark Ages,* New York, 1904, p. 69.

30. See *Timon*, 10.

31. Also of other post-Aristotelian philosophies. Compare *Menander,* 549K and 556K, English translation by F. G. Allinson, in *The Loeb Classical Library,* New York and London, 1921.

32. *Philopseudes,* or *The Maker and Lover of Lies.*

33. See below, p. 177, and add St. Patrick's extermination of snakes, etc., in Ireland, modelled after Lucian.

34. Cf. Franz Cumont, *op. cit.,* especially pp. 8 and 23.

35. See photographs, fronting page 109, of the coin of Ionopolis (= Abonūteichos, cf. Pape, *Griech. Eigennamen, s. v.*) and of the bronze statuette of the snake-god, Glykon, now in the Boston Museum of Fine Arts. See Museum *Bulletin,* Vol. II. 2, 1904.

36. Compare the curious mechanism found in the excavations at ancient Corinth by which, as interpreted by Director B. H. Hill of the American School of Classical Studies at Athens, an unseen " prophet " could give oracular answers through a concealed passage.

37. For references see Allinson, *Lucian, op. cit.*, pp. xv and 205–6.

38. *Odyssey*, VII. 115 ff.

39. For further details, obligations to Antonius Diogenes, and coincidences with the *Arabian Nights*, see below, p. 124.

40. Unless we assume that it was borrowed, *en bloc,* from the lost Comedy of Antiphanes, see below, p. 122. See also pp. 161, 180.

41. See below, pp. 127 ff.

42. See illustration opposite page 109.

43. For discussion of the testimony of Athenagoras, Philostratus, Eusebius, and Ammianus Marcellinus, see Allinson, *Lucian, op. cit.*, pp. 202–204.

44. Sandys (see Bibliography), Vol. I, pp. 320–321, however, is inclined to follow the opinion of Hemsterhuis that Lucian does not refer to Pollux.

45. For a happy paraphrase of the untranslatable blunders, see the version by the Fowlers (see Bibliography).

46. *E.g.,* The *Pseudopurist* or *Solecist.*

47. See Harmon, *Lucian*, Vol. I, p. 395.

48. For Lucian's use or ridicule of predecessors, see below, p. 124, note; for his *Vera Historia*, see Rohde, p. 196 (cf. Bibliography), for his preëminence in parody, cf. Rohde, p. 206, note to 210, for *Thule*, p. 260; and for Lucian's relation to Hesiod, Comedy, etc., and to the mediaeval Utopias, see " The Greek Land of Cockaigne," by Campbell Bonner, *Transactions of the American Philological Association*, XLI. 175–185 (1910).

49. See, for example, in *True Story*, II. 28, the mockery of the prophylactic given to Odysseus by Hermes, *Od.*, X. 288 ff.

50. See below, p. 185, for Nansen's comparison with the Norse " Ginnungagap."

51. Accepted by Croiset, *op. cit.*, see pp. 63 and 204; also H. W. Smyth, *Greek Dialects*, Oxford, 1894, pp. 116–119, for Lucian's Ionism.

52. Translated (expurgated) by E. J. Smith in *Selections from Lucian*, Harper's, New York, 1892.

53. For pedigree of the " Ass," see *The Metamorphoses*

NOTES

Ascribed to Lucius of Patrae, by B. F. Perry (Princeton dissertation, 1919). Sandys (*op. cit.*), Vol. I, p. 310, accepts the *Ass* as Lucianic, as does Von Christ (cf. Bibliography), 2nd part, 2nd half, p. 736.

54. Cf., *inter alios,* the critical panegyric of M. Croiset, *op. cit.,* pp. 385–389, 291–296, and G. E. B. Saintsbury's verdict: *A History of Criticism,* Vol. I, p. 150, *et passim.*

55. Assuming that Antonius lived as early as the first Christian century. For detailed discussion of the extracts from Antonius in Photius: Μυριοβίβλιον ἢ Βιβλιοθήκη, as well as for other sources, from Homer to Theopompus on to Plutarch, and also for traces of far-flung oriental tales, see E. Rohde, pp. 242–250, 260 ff.

56. M. Croiset, *op. cit.,* p. 70 and note.

57. See, for Lucretius, Franz Cumont, *After Life in Roman Paganism,* pp. 8, 9. (Cumont's suggestion might be reenforced by Lucian's own transliteration σακερδῶτες, *Alex.,* 48), also p. 67 for the obvious rehearsal in *Philops.* 31, of Pliny's ghost story; for Virgil and the cornel-tree of *Aen.* iii, see C. S. Jerram: *Luciani Vera Historia,* Oxford, 1892, I, 120; and, *ibidem,* note on *V. H.,* I. 37 for Juvenal; and note to *V. H.,* II. 33 for Ovid; for *all* of these Roman authors (except Pliny), see H. W. L. Hime, *Lucian the Syrian Satirist,* London, New York, and Bombay, 1900, Appendix, pp. 92–95, *i.e.,* thirteen parallel passages (some more convincing than others); for Ovid, see also Croiset, *op. cit.,* p. 311; for Tacitus, see Sandys, *op. cit.,* II, p. 309; for Plautus, cf. *Trinummus,* Act. iv., Sc. 4 for some direct or indirect connection with Lucian's *Icaromenippus.* Also *Lucian's True History,* p. 9, by Chas. Whibley, London, 1894.

58. *Ars Amat.,* II. 687 ff.

59. See Blümner (cf. Bibliography).

60. E. A. Gardner, *A Handbook of Greek Sculpture,* New York and London, 1897, p. 3.

61. For the two types of the *Europa* story and for *Andromeda* with details and citations, see Allinson, *op. cit.,* p. 185, notes, and pp. 181–184; cf. E. S. Hartland, *Legend of Perseus,* London, 1894–96.

62. See above, p. 107.

63. Madvig's enticing emendation, *Piscator*, 39, τὴν πτερωτὴν for τήν γε πρώτην.

64. Cf. Förster, p. 18 (see Bibliography), for Fonzio, Benvenuto Garofalo, Luca, Signorelli; p. 20 for the Alexander-Roxana subject; and foll. pp. for many other suggestions.

65. For specimens of Holbein's "Dance of Death," see frontispiece.

66. The complicated Holbein question is discussed in *The (N. Y.) Nation*, Nov. 19, 1903, in a review of a re-issue of the Bell-Macmillan ed. of the *Dance of Death*. The original drawings, now accessible, show "that they are by more than one hand." . . . "It is demonstrable that the designer was not always, and hence possibly not at all, the draughtsman for the wood-engraver." The woodcuts of the original Lyons edition of 1538 should be compared.

67. For details of the Lübeck painting, see p. 19 of the *Dance of Death in Painting and Print*, by T. Tindall Wildridge, London, 1887, an inexpensive illustrated booklet which gives, *inter alia*, some 30 examples in England, France, Germany and Switzerland of the "Dance of Death" in painting or (occasionally) in sculpture on bridges or in houses, churchyards, and cloisters. For the motif itself, firmly naturalized in Europe independent of any literary tradition, see the scenes in *Death's Jest Book*, by Thos. Beddoes (cf. p. 179, below). For its early appearance in literature Rentsch (see Bibliography), p. 25, cites from Thibaut de Marly in the 13th century, thus *antedating* the passage cited by Wildridge, *op. cit.*, p. 13, from *Piers Plowman* (1350).

68. See Chapter I, pp. 10–12. See also Hardin Craig, "Dryden's Lucian," in *Classical Philology*, xvi. 141–163 (1921).

69. Cf. Saintsbury, *Hist. Criticism*, I. 474.

70. Cf. Sandys, *op. cit.*, *versus* Pauly-Wissowa, article "Alciphron."

71. See W. C. Wright, *Philostratus, Introd.*, p. xiv, in *The Loeb Classical Library*.

72. *Orat.*, No. XXV (*Teubner* text).

NOTES

73. For Libanius, see *Introd.*, p. 335, to W. C. Wright's edition of *Eunapius* (*The Loeb Class. Libr.*).

74. Cf. J. Rentsch, *Das Totengespräch in der Litteratur*, Plauen, 1895, p. 17, note.

75 *Lives of the Philosophers and Sophists*, ed. cit., The *Loeb Classical Lib.*, p. 348.

76. See K. Krumbacher (cf. Bibliography), p. 495, § 211 and Rentsch, *op. cit.*, p. 21.

77. Sandys, *op. cit.*, I. p. 491.

78. Sandys, *op. cit.*, p. 399.

79. Krumbacher, *op. cit.*, pp. 526–536, § 219.

80. See detailed résumé in Rentsch, *op. cit.*, pp. 21 ff. Also see Krumbacher, p. 218, for Psellus as Lucianic pamphleteer.

81. Cf. Krumbacher, *op. cit.*, pp. 492–495, and Rentsch, *op. cit.*, p. 22.

82. See Krumbacher, *op. cit.*, p. 756, § 313 (13), and Sandys, *op. cit.*, I. 410.

83. The content of this dialogue is accessible in Bolderman's dissertation, see above, note 15, or in *Notices et Extraits des Manuscrits de la Bibliothèque impériale*, 1810, Art. 37.

84. Cf. F. Schumacher, *De Johanne Katrario Luciani imitatore*, Bonn, 1908, who decides for the later dating.

85. Sandys, *op. cit.*, p. 36.

86. See R. Förster, *op. cit.*, p. 8. This particular dialogue had a great vogue among imitators of Lucian.

87. See G. Gregory Smith, *The Transition Period*, New York, 1900, pp. 140 ff. and pp. 306 and 387; also Förster, *op. cit.*, pp. 9, 10.

88. See below, pp. 161, 180, the different conceptions by Molière and Bulwer.

89. G. B. E. Saintsbury, *Earlier Renaissance*, New York, 1901, p. 24, note.

90. Cf. Saintsbury, *ibidem*, p. 406, and p. 72.

91. Cf. *Cicero* by J. C. Rolfe, in the Series, *Our Debt to Greece and Rome*, pp. 137 ff.

92. His strictures upon a *previous* (unnamed) translator, see *Epistles*, ed. by Nichols (cf. Bibliography), Vol. I, 408,

are interesting in connection with the Shakespeare tradition. He is certainly not referring to Boiardo's *Il Timone,* see above, p. 142.

93. Cf. *Epistles, op. cit.,* II. p. 49.

94. *Epistles,* cccclxiii.

95. Cf. J. A. Froude, *Life and Letters of Erasmus,* New York, 1896, p. 220.

96. *Epistle to the Bishop of Chartres,* No. 179, Nichols, *op. cit.,* I. p. 415.

97. *Colloq.,* No. xiii, ed. London, 1725, L'Estrange (Thos. Brown), p. 199: " This story . . . outdoes Menander's *Phasma.*"

98. *Colloq.,* vii, *op. cit.*

99. *Colloq.,* Patrick's ed., London, 1750, p. 380.

100. Cf. Froude, *op. cit.,* pp. 81 ff.

101. Froude, *op. cit.,* p. 86. See Nichols, *op. cit.,* I. p. 404, who corrects Froude's error, *op. cit.,* p. 300, in attributing to Erasmus this letter by More. This somewhat distorts Froude's estimate.

102. See Saintsbury, *Earlier Renaissance,* p. 86.

103. Holbein illustrated More's *Utopia* as well as Erasmus's *Encomium Moriae.*

104. Cf. Saintsbury, *Earl. Ren.,* p. 92.

105. See Saintsbury, *Earl. Ren.,* p. 81 and pp. 99, 100 for résumé. See also Förster, *op. cit.,* p. 14, where Pirckheimer is accepted as the author.

106. For a good, if nationalistic, account of their contributions, see Förster, *op. cit.,* where Erasmus, however, is nonchalantly listed (p. 7) as a German! For Erasmus's attitude to his own (Dutch) language and his own statement that he did not even *understand German,* see Nichols, I. p. 153, and Froude, *op. cit.,* p. 306.

107. See Rentsch, *op. cit.,* p. 23.

108. Also, *loc. cit.,* other contemporary writers, Spanish, German, Italian.

109. See Sandys, *op. cit.,* II. p. 267.

110. For both Budé and Rabelais and their use of Lucian, see Sandys, *op. cit.,* II. pp. 170–173, 182.

111. Saintsbury, *Earlier Ren.,* p. 226; also *Hist. of Crit.,* II. p. 516.

112. *Essays and Studies, op. cit.,* pp. 312–313.

113. For Lucian in Rabelais, cf. Sandys, *op. cit.,* II. pp. 183–184.

114. See Saintsbury, *Hist. of French Literature* (cf. Bibliography), pp. 231–236.

115. See W. S. Fox, " Sources of the Grave-scene in Hamlet," p. 76 (see below, note 120).

116. *Cambr. Hist. Eng. Lit.,* IV, p. 404. *This* is probably the first English trans. of Lucian in use.

117. C. H. Herford, cited by Fox, " Grave-scene in Hamlet," p. 77 (see note 120).

118. *Volpone,* Act. I, pp. 11–13, of the " Mermaid " edition.

119. Probably written by Fletcher only, see C. M. Gayley, *Beaumont the Dramatist,* New York, 1914, pp. 301 ff.

120. See two monographs by W. Sherwood Fox, " Sources of the Grave-scene in Hamlet " (Part I, *Trans. Roy. Soc. Canada,* pp. 71–80, Vol. xvii, 3rd series, 1923, and Part II, " Lucian in the Grave-scene of Hamlet," *Philological Quarierly,* II. 132–141 (1923). To these two valuable monographs the present writer is indebted for various details already cited. Mr. Fox cites, correlates and supplements the many references to Lucian in the *Cambr. Hist. Eng. Lit.,* (q. v.) His detailed argument should be read in full, especially as regards the translation into English of Lucian by John Rastell, brother-in-law of Sir Thos. More. This is significant for Shakespeare.

121. See the paper by Professor Parrott, London, 1923, " The Timon of Athens," where this play is dissected and definite portions are attributed to Shakespeare, to Chapman and to a reviser " X." In the only significant Lucianic reminiscence (among twelve in all) Mr. Parrott sees Chapman's hand.

122. Cf. Rentsch, *op. cit.,* p. 27, for good summary. Also for the Spanish Jesuit Gracian and for various German successors.

123. *Hist. of Crit.,* I. p. 150.

124. Cf. many other references made by Rentsch, *op. cit.,* not noted here with the others added to his lists.

125. See the admirable monograph by **Hardin Craig**, in *Classical Philology*, XVI. 141–63 (1921), on " Dryden's Lucian." Many of his references should be followed up if any approach to completeness were possible in this sketch. At about this time there was a " bumper " crop of translators of Lucian and of dialogues of varying merit, reflecting or refracting Lucianic influence. Mr. Craig's detailed study of English versions begins with the admirable translation by Francis Hickes (pub. in 1634, and, for the *Vera Historia*, reissued in a beautiful volume, privately printed in 1894 with an introduction by Charles Whibley), and is invaluable as a basis for a chronological appraisal of Lucian's influence, *after* this date, in English literature. Especially interesting are his comments on the " clever and impertinent coxcomb," Ferdinand Spence, whose unacknowledged borrowing, with copious perversions, from the already perverted, but popular, French paraphrase by D'Ablancourt (called, by courtesy, a " translation ") makes his own " traducing " a " third remove," to speak mildly, from the Lucianic realities. In regard to a translation, however, previous to the translation by Hickes, see note 120, *supra*.

Part III of Mr. Craig's paper contains a list of the 27 translators in this collection, known as " Dryden's Lucian," with a most helpful commentary on the date available for each and on the varying merits of their respective shares in the work. The mere number alone is suggestive of the contemporary popularity of Lucian.

126. Rentsch, *op. cit.*, pp. 29–31 and his note 35, adds the names of other writers of dialogues who openly claimed both Fontenelle and Lucian as models. Amongst others, Bordelon, in his preface to *Caractères naturels des hommes*, La Haye, 1692, is especially explicit as to his indebtedness, and, in *Molière Comedien aux Champs élisées*, he also imitated Fontenelle's *Jugement de Paris*.

127. See note, p. 249, C. R. Williams's admirable edition, *Selections from Lucian*, Boston, 1882.

128. For summary of Lucianic motifs, see Rentsch, *op. cit.*, p. 38.

129. *Op. cit.*, p. 378. For other critical comparisons, see

NOTES

B. L. Gildersleeve, *op. cit.*, p. 312, for Lucian, Rabelais and Voltaire; Saintsbury, *History of Criticism*, II. pp. 517 ff., where Voltaire furnishes the point of departure for comparing the others; J. A. Froude, *Short Studies on Great Subjects*, 3rd series, New York, 1877, pp. 210–240; and J. Rentsch, " Lucian and Voltaire " (see Bibliography).

130. See p. xxiv of Charles Whibley's (*op. cit.*) introduction to *Lucian: True History*.

131. See above, note 129. To these commentators add Lytton Strachey, in *Collected Essays: Books and Characters*, New York, 1922. Cf. " Voltaire and England," " Voltaire's Tragedies," " Voltaire and Frederick the Great "; also a dialogue, hitherto unpublished, between " Moses, Diogenes, and Mr. Loke," which is Lucianic enough in its pessimism.

132. *Earlier Ren.*, p. 85.

133. Vol. XLV, No. X.

134. See notes to Jerram's stimulating school edition of the *Vera Historia*, Oxford, 1892.

135. But cf. Erich Schmidt, *Lessing*,[3] Berlin, 1909, pp. 99, 100.

136. Nos. 360, 361, 362.

137. See H. W. L. Hime, *Lucian the Syrian Satirist*, London and New York, 1900, p. 92; see above, note 57.

138. See Gildersleeve, *op. cit.*, p. 344; also Grillparzer, *Studien III, zur Literatur*, 370, 1842, who says: " Der Keim zu Chamisso's *Peter Schlemihl* liegt wohl in diesem Luzianischen Dialog." Professor R. McB. Mitchell calls my attention to a triple use of Lucian, Chamisso's and Hoffman's ideas being interwoven by Jacques Offenbach: *Contes d'Hoffman*, Paris, 1881.

139. See Gosse's introd., p. xxxviii, *Poetical Works of Thos. Lovell Beddoes*, London, 1890.

140. A reminiscence, probably accidental, of the fluttering hopes, fears, etc., in Lucian's *Charon* is suggested for Dickens: *Dombey and Son*, Gadshill ed., New York, 1897. Vol. II, Chapter xlvii.

141. *De Lapsu*, 3, where the name is spelled Phei*l*ippides.

NOTES

142. Riverside Press ed. *Dramas,* p. 204. This reminiscence noted by Professor Hastings.

143. *Third Series,* pp. 210–240.

144. See above, p. 140.

145. *Cambr. Hist. Eng. Lit.,* IX. p. 179.

146. New ed. (enlarged), 1900, London.

147. *In Northern Mists,* I. p. 366, New York, 1911, Nansen emphasizes, of course, the fact that no written MS. of Lucian was then accessible. This account by Saint Brandan he dates (Vol. I, p. 359) before 1100 A.D. For the " Legend of Saint Brandan " and the genius of the Celts " for the Aristophanic blending of beauty with enormous laughter," see W. P. Ker, *The Dark Ages,* New York, 1909, pp. 61 ff.

148. Vol. II. p. 150.

149. *Gaisford Greek Prose,* 1922, Oxford: Basil Blackwell, citations in *Spectator,* Oct. 28, 1922.

CONDENSED BIBLIOGRAPHY

Translations:

HARMON, A. M., *Lucian with an English Translation,* in *The Loeb Classical Library,* London and New York, 1913 — . When completed in eight volumes, the best and most accessible edition of the Greek text with translation.

FOWLER, H. W., AND F. G., *The Works of Lucian of Samosata* (translation complete with exceptions specified), 4 vols. Oxford, 1905. Contains conspectus of titles in Greek, Latin and English.

For other translations in Latin, English, French, German, etc., previous to 1905, see bibliography in Allinson's *Lucian* (*infra*), and also discussion in notes above. The translation of some titles has been borrowed from William Tooke's quaint, though often inaccurate, version, London, 1820.

The four works following give a vivid picture, full length or in miniature, of Lucian:

1. CROISET, MAURICE, *La Vie et les Oeuvres de Lucien.* Paris, 1882.
2. GILDERSLEEVE, B. L., *Essays and Studies.* Baltimore, 1880.
3. LANG, ANDREW, *Letters to Dead Authors.* New York, 1893.
4. SOMMERBRODT, J. W. E., *Ausgewählte Schriften des Lucian.* Berlin, 1872.

For Lucian's influence on successors (in addition to works cited once in Notes), for his relation to art; for his Greek:

ALLINSON, F. G., *Lucian, Selected Writings.* Boston and New York, 1905. (Especially pp. xx–xlii.)

BIBLIOGRAPHY

BLÜMNER, HUGO, *Archaeologische Studien zu Lucian*. Breslau, 1867. (With its full citation of works of art, mentioned by Lucian, this monograph has been much used.)

CHABERT, S., *L'Atticisme de Lucien*. Paris, 1897.

VON CHRIST, W. (Schmid, W., and Stahlin, O.), *Griechische Litteratur* [6]. Munich, 1924.

CROISET, A. AND M., *Histoire de la Littérature Grecque*. Paris, 1899. (Vol. V., pp. 583–616.)

FÖRSTER, RICHARD, *Lucian in der Renaissance*. Kiel, 1886.

KRUMBACHER, K., *Byzantinische Litteratur* [2]. Munich, 1897.

NICHOLS, F. M., *Epistles of Erasmus*. 3 vols. London and New York, 1901–18. (For Erasmus's comments on Lucian, see Vol. I., pp. 370, 391, 403, 406, 408, 409, 415, 422, and II, 65, 133, 204, 658.)

RENTSCH, J., *Lucianstudien*. Plauen, 1895. This includes " Lucian und Voltaire " and " Das Totengespräch in der Litteratur."

ROHDE, E., *Der griechische Roman* [3] (enlarged by W. Schmid). Leipzig, 1914.

SAINTSBURY, G. E. B., *A History of Criticism* [3]. 3 vols. New York and Edinburgh, 1908.

——, *Earlier Renaissance*. New York, 1901.

——, *A Short History of French Literature* [6]. Oxford, 1901.

SANDYS, J. E., *A History of Classical Scholarship*. 3 vols. Cambridge, 1903–1908.

SCHMID, W., *Der Atticismus*. Stuttgart, 1887–1897.

Our Debt to Greece and Rome

AUTHORS AND TITLES

AUTHORS AND TITLES

DATE DUE

SE 20'82			

GAYLORD   PRINTED IN U.S.A.